*Critical Guides to French Texts*

EDITED BY ROGER LITTLE, WOLFGANG VAN EMDEN,
DAVID WILLIAMS

RACINE

# Mithridate

**Henry Phillips**

Lecturer in French in the
University of Cambridge and
Fellow of Emmanuel College

**Grant & Cutler Ltd**
1990

© Grant & Cutler Ltd
1990

ISBN 0-7293-0317-9

349996

I.S.B.N. 84-599-2929-9

DEPÓSITO LEGAL: V. 250 - 1990

Printed in Spain by
Artes Gráficas Soler, S. A., Valencia

for

GRANT & CUTLER LTD
55-57, GREAT MARLBOROUGH STREET, LONDON W1V 2AY

*To Dick and Doris Phillips*

# Contents

# *Prefatory Note*

ITALICISED numerals in parentheses, followed where appropriate by a page number, refer to the numbered items in the Bibliography at the end of this volume.

The text to which all references have been made is the Nouveaux Classiques Larousse edition of *Mithridate,* with introduction, notes etc. by Madeleine Brunelle. Other available editions are listed in the Bibliography.

# Introduction

T R A G E D Y possesses an aura of mystique such as no other dramatic genre. It concerns, at least in its classical manifestation, the action of kings, queens or of characters whose rank places them in situations of an exceptional nature. The heroic action of the tragedy often evokes savage feelings of hatred and revenge, whose import may be enhanced by elevation to a plane above that of common humanity, whether this involves divine intervention or historical inevitability. Tragedy, then, offers a vision of humanity in the world. But the tragic concept is what we abstract from tragic praxis. Tragedies are written for an audience and take place in the theatre. Tragedy is drama.

I have therefore chosen in this critical guide to *Mithridate* to concentrate mostly on how the play promotes action and how action elicits a response from the spectator. This can be observed at a variety of levels: structure, speech and character (see chapters 1, 2, 3 and 5). The concepts of space and time are the subject of chapter 4 which concentrates in particular on geographical space and the place represented by the stage in relation to the stage space itself.

The adoption of an approach based on purely dramatic concepts inevitably entails the recurrence of certain themes from time to time but, I hope, in sufficiently distinct contexts for their significance to be enhanced rather than reduced. In fact this may serve to demonstrate the ultimately convergent nature of any single element of a text. Such is the case with the notion of revelation in the tragedy, which is relevant to structure, language, and character. Throughout my discussion of *Mithridate* runs the central concept of what I have termed 'control', by which I mean the ability of the characters to apprehend fully their situation and to impose their authority upon it.

The confines imposed by the format and by my mode of analysis have led to the exclusion of a number of considerations. Critical approaches to Racine have been the subject of much controversy over the years but I have not sought to enter that particular arena. Items *1, 2, 4* and *24* in the Bibliography will act among others as useful and stimulating compensation. Equally I have not explored the historical situation of *Mithridate* (see item *23*), nor Racine's use of sources. Michael O'Regan provides an excellent account of the latter in his book (item *21*), the first individual study of the play.

Rather, my intention here, and in saying this I offer no polemical comment, has been to offer not only a close analysis of *Mithridate* but a possible reading of any Racinian text.

# 1
# Structure and Effect

L I K E any playwright, the tragedian must first and foremost adopt a strategy which will involve the spectator throughout the tragic action. For tragedy contains emotions which are at their greatest level of intensity. Emotion in itself is not self-sustaining in the theatre. In order to be effective, and, above all to persuade, it must be articulated through the organisation the playwright brings to the action by means of the structure of his work. There is, then, before all else, a primary level of response according to which we perceive the tragic vision. A playwright has therefore, in the words of J. L. Styan, to force upon our attention this or that speech or deed (*33*, p. 53). I should like in this chapter to explore some ways in which Racine achieves his effects at this primary level of response and in which, within the classical medium of tragedy in seventeenth-century France, he maintains our interest throughout *Mithridate*.

Indeed one of the most important aspects of dramatic action is its movement, its progression. Our perception of this movement is not only retrospective, that is to say in the way we compare point B with point A in order to identify what has changed. The action at any given moment also projects us forwards by arousing our expectations and by creating suspense, two elements of drama to which Racine pays great attention. His dramatic practice in this regard can be illustrated by an analysis of the first two acts of the play.

Racine does not delay in taking us to the heart of the conflict: Mithridate

> [...] laisse, après lui, pour venger son trépas,
> Deux fils infortunés qui ne s'accordent pas.    (13-14)

Xipharès then informs Arbate of Pharnace's intentions towards Monime and his own love for her. Racine thus creates
through the details imparted to us a climate of expectancy,
first in Act I, scene 2 when Xipharès meets Monime, and
then in Act I, scene 3 when Pharnace joins them. Our
curiosity is aroused as to the manner in which these three
characters will approach the rivalry between them.

The nature of our expectation, which in the first few
scenes revolves around the love interest of the two brothers,
is radically transformed by the news of Mithridate's return.
The scene between the two brothers (I,5) now serves to
inform us of the king's character, particularly his ferocity
(344-52) and his jealousy. Pharnace warns Xipharès that

> Amant avec transport, mais jaloux sans retour,
> Sa haine va toujours plus loin que son amour.   (353-54)

The betrayal of Pharnace and Xipharès, as constituted by
their declarations of love to Monime, thus raises the drama to
a more critical level, as they are henceforward both rivals to
the king.

At this stage Racine leaves the spectator eagerly awaiting
the appearance of Mithridate. The spectator is however
denied immediate satisfaction, for Monime opens Act II
rather than the king. One can account for this procedure in
two ways. First, Racine has not yet provided all the elements necessary for the full impact of Mithridate's presence.
Monime must declare her love for Xipharès (although it is
implicit in her remark in 221-22), so that Pharnace, Xipharès
and Monime can all be implicated in the betrayal of the king.
Secondly, the delay in introducing Mithridate allows the
spectator's feeling of expectation to reassert itself. In fact,
Racine's dramatic strategy in withholding the appearance of
Mithridate illustrates other dramatic concerns. One might
have thought that, given the exposure of rivalry in Act I, the
moment had arrived for a confrontation between two major
characters. Instead, for the sake of *vraisemblance* (and *bien-
séance*), Racine interpolates a short scene where the king
admonishes his two sons who have presumably gone to meet

him at the port (i.e. he should not be seen to arrive in his palace alone), after which Mithridate recounts his defeat to Arbate (II,3), and questions the latter closely about the conduct of Xipharès, Pharnace and Monime in his absence. Act II, scene 3, of course, also sets up the error Mithridate makes about Monime's relationship with Pharnace. Indeed, another reason can be adduced for delaying the encounter between Monime and Mithridate, namely that the spectator must witness at first hand the ferocity of the king in Act II, scenes 2-3 in order to increase our expectation with regard to Act II, scene 4.

So far I have been concerned with the notion of expectation which at one level clearly contains within itself the notion of suspense. However suspense makes its greatest impact at those moments where a pause interrupts the action, or, in the case of drama, the performance. Importance attaches therefore to the way in which each act terminates the segment of the action allotted to it. While the creation of suspense in this way is a convention of classical drama, it is none the less interesting to examine how Racine observed it.

Act I ends, as I have shown, with the reported return of Mithridate to Nymphée. This event raises a number of dramatic questions to which we expect the answers in the following act. Will the brothers and Monime be able to suppress what has occurred between them? How will Mithridate react to finding both his sons in Nymphée at the same time? The end of Act II provides us with the most open question in the play as far as the further advance of the action is concerned, for Xipharès has at the same time been ordered to guard Monime and to avoid her presence, the first order coming from Mithridate and the second from Monime. How can this be achieved? No clues whatsoever exist as to what Xipharès's solution will be, until his speech in Act III, scene 1, after Mithridate has unveiled his audacious plan to march on Rome, in which he appeals to his father to be allowed to leave the Bosphorus. Our feelings at the close of Act III are more firmly directed in that Mithridate has now discovered Xipharès's love for Monime, and determines to continue his dissimulating conduct. What fate will therefore befall

Xipharès and Monime? A similar question arises after Act
IV, although in this case the problem of a solution is
compounded by the invasion of the Romans. The fate of all
the characters, but more specifically Monime, is now thrown
into the balance.

In the previous discussion I have referred to the fact that
at different stages of the action dramatic questions are raised
which require answers if the spectator's expectations are to be
fully satisfied. Of course, these answers are not always immediately forthcoming. In Racinian tragedy as a whole a solution to the problems posed in the first act is constantly
deferred in the course of the action. In *Mithridate* the deferral
of a solution depends initially on an act of concealment,
where information is suppressed and subsequently revealed.
The pace of that revelation determines in large part the
emotional tension of the action.

The initial act of concealment is that of Arbate in Act II,
scene 3. He knows that Xipharès loves Monime and that he
intends to declare himself to her. Arbate even encourages him
(127). When interrogated by Mithridate Arbate avoids giving
any direct indication of Xipharès's feelings: his words are in
fact deliberately ambiguous:

> Son frère, au moins jusqu'à ce jour,
> Seigneur, dans ses desseins n'a point marqué d'amour.   (497-98)

Arbate suppresses the information that Xipharès has spoken
of his love for Monime, while he in part tells the truth (i.e.
that Xipharès has come to Nymphée to protect his inheritance).

From this moment, the effectiveness of the dramatic
action at the primary level of response lies in our perception
of Mithridate's passage from ignorance of what has occurred
to knowledge. Moreover, the deferral of a solution, itself
dependent on knowledge, is equally crucial, since discovery
and revelation will have consequences for others. The structure of *Mithridate* is, then, principally one of revelation and
delay to the extent that the deferral of a solution underpins

the emotional climate of the tragedy both for the characters and the spectator.

The idea of deferral implies either obstacles to the full disclosure of previous events or reasons which prevent a character from acting resolutely according to the knowledge he possesses. Both elements are present in *Mithridate*. In order to delay Mithridate's full realisation of the truth, Racine has recourse to a conventional device. Mithridate misunderstands the meaning of Monime's unenthusiastic attitude to his opening speech in Act II, scene 4 (547-50). Mithridate's error concerning which of his two sons she is in love with persists at least until Act III, scene 2, when, after Pharnace's outburst (994-98), he begins to suspect that it is Xipharès and not Pharnace that Monime prefers. His error is, of course, initially dependent on Arbate's reference to Pharnace's approach to Monime (491-94). The process of Mithridate's discovery of the truth occupies the remaining scenes of Act III.

But Mithridate's realisation of the real nature of events prior to his return to Nymphée leads in turn to a set of revelations for other characters. For Mithridate's trickery and dissimulation have now to be brought to light. Monime suspects Mithridate of a deceptive manœuvre in Act IV, scene 1, a suspicion confirmed by Xipharès in Act IV, scene 2. It remains for Xipharès to discover that Monime was the one who betrayed him, as it turns out, inadvertently. The final element of disclosure occurs in Act IV, scene 4 when Monime forces the king to acknowledge implicitly his dishonesty. The principal characters (Pharnace has since moved into the background) have now all achieved a state of enlightenment about events. There is left the revenge of the king, the exact nature of which has yet to be divulged.

Two further devices of deferral intervene at this point. The first comprises Mithridate's hesitation in enacting his revenge in Act IV, scene 5. His reluctance to act swiftly derives from his recognition that, if he is to defeat Rome, he has need of his son. He even contemplates allowing Xipharès to marry Monime, thus foreshadowing his later decision.

Act IV, scene 5 indeed ends on a note of self-interrogation: 'De ce trouble fatal par où dois-je sortir?' (1421).

The second device which postpones any decision on the fate of Xipharès and Monime is the escape of Pharnace and the unexplained conduct of Xipharès when Mithridate's soldiers mutiny (IV,6), followed by the Roman invasion of Nymphée (IV,7). The act concludes with whispered orders to Arcas and the clear implication that Monime's fate at least has been sealed. The exact nature of this revenge is disclosed in Act V, scene 7 and Mithridate's final decision in the very last scene of the play.

One cannot however avoid the conclusion that the structure of *Mithridate* fails to sustain a constant level of emotional intensity. Inevitably a comparison suggests itself between *Mithridate* and *Phèdre,* two tragedies which deal with the consequences of a return from the dead. The report of Mithridate's death and of Thésée's disappearance both provoke confessions which would have otherwise been suppressed. Each tragedy, based on a structure of revelation and delay, then explores the gradual disclosure of what has taken place. But the events of *Phèdre* are more charged with passion, especially since Phèdre is already married to Thésée and has confessed her love to one who reluctantly hears her. Moreover, Thésée returns much later in the action (there is more of consequence to reveal in *Phèdre* than in *Mithridate*), since the rumour that he is alive is reported in Act II, scene 6, his reappearance not coming until Act III, scene 4. In addition the revelation of events in *Phèdre* is complete only at Phèdre's confession in the final scene of the play, which leaves the confirmation of Hippolyte's innocence to the end, at which point Thésée becomes fully aware of what has happened. Mithridate discovers the most important details by Act III, scene 6, after which the play requires other devices to continue the action. Act V of *Mithridate* is the weakest. The king's revenge is known in scene 2, rescinded in scene 3, whereupon Racine has recourse to a report of the battle containing none of the thematic significance of the 'récit de Théramène'. Lastly, Mithridate moves relatively straightforwardly from discovery to revenge, whereas Thésée's revenge *precedes* discovery, thus allowing for a greater measure of emotional impact. I shall return to the question of weaknesses in Racine's dramatic strategy in *Mithridate* at various stages in the following chapters.

One of my concerns in the preceding pages has been the way in which Racine maintains the spectator's interest, particularly at the level of expectation and suspense. In this regard, the demands of the classical form, especially as Racine conceives it, are greater than in many other dramatic traditions in view of the small number of principal characters involved in the action. After *La Thébaïde* and *Alexandre* Racine operates with three or four protagonists, *Mithridate* being of the former variety. Certainly Pharnace is a fourth principal character in the sense that he is Mithridate's son. But he is no longer dramatically significant after Act III, scene 2. Perhaps another weakness of the play is indeed that the brothers' rivalry and Pharnace's love for Monime are insufficiently exploited. Pharnace is in fact alone with another character only once in the play, with Xipharès in Act I, scene 5.

The problem of the classical form in the terms just described is thus the avoidance of monotony and repetition. Of course, the *confident(e)* provides an element of variation in tone, whereby the main characters enjoy both an intimacy without danger (*Britannicus* being the exception) and the possibility of disclosing feelings inappropriate in other sorts of confrontation. The best and most consistent use of the *confident(e)* is undoubtedly *Andromaque,* although J. C. Lapp has argued that Racine's first major tragedy stands more or less alone in exploiting the *confident(e)* in this way (see *12,* chapter iii). In *Mithridate* the *confident* character appears twice in Act I, three times in Act II, not at all in Act III, but more frequently in Acts IV-V, although sometimes simply as a messenger. Arbate's role is of some interest given that he is the *confident* of both Xipharès and Mithridate. His role is indeed crucial in that he withholds a vital piece of information from Mithridate in Act II, scene 3. But, at the same time, he cannot be accused of duplicity, unlike Narcisse in *Britannicus.*

With the action concentrated around a small number of characters it will be interesting to explore precisely how Racine maintains our interest in the tragic action. To begin with, it is remarkable on how comparatively few occasions individual sets of characters meet each other, that is to say, how infrequently the same two characters are together in the same scene with no other in attendance.

The action of *Mithridate* focuses mainly on the relationships between Xipharès and Monime, Monime and Mithridate, and Mithridate and Xipharès. The relationship between Pharnace and Mithridate possesses less interest than that between Xipharès and his father. Pharnace is almost a device serving Mithridate's misunderstanding and acts to highlight the contrast between his own treachery and the political fidelity of Xipharès. Pharnace appears in only five scenes in all. If we return to Xipharès, Monime and Mithridate, we find that Xipharès shares six out of a total of twenty-nine scenes with Monime, of which only three (I,2; II,6; IV,2) can be considered intimate. Mithridate confronts Monime in three scenes (II,4; III,5; IV,4) and appears with her on two other occasions, in Act III, scene 5 when only Mithridate speaks, and in the final scene of the play. In only one of the five scenes in which Xipharès meets Mithridate are they alone together (III,3).

The absence of quantitative variety in meetings between the characters has therefore to be replaced by a qualitative variety if the spectator's interest is to be maintained. In other words, in the second and subsequent meetings between the same two characters, some progression in the action should have taken place, and the terms of the characters' discussion altered in a significant way. Given how these confrontations are spaced in the course of the play, each confrontation between the same characters must be more meaningful than the last and itself contribute to the forward movement of the action.

Let us look at the differences between scenes containing the same characters through the example of Monime and Xipharès. Naturally each scene in which they appear takes its place in the action as a whole, and what takes place between the characters when they are together is determined by events that have occurred meanwhile. There is thus an interlocking relationship between those meetings involving Monime and Xipharès together, and those involving other combinations of characters, especially that of Monime and Mithridate. The different consequences following from one confrontation to the next account for the movement of the action and the development of relationships.

Monime and Xipharès share three scenes of intimacy (I,2; II,6; and IV,2). In the first of these, Xipharès declares his love to Monime. Monime herself only hints at her affection for Xipharès (221-22). Between this and their next meeting in Act II, scene 6, considerable developments have taken place: Mithridate has returned, received a cool response from Monime and has accused her of loving Pharnace. Consequently, Monime finds it necessary to defend herself against this charge to Xipharès himself, especially since it was made in his presence. Under the pressure of defending herself, she declares her love for the young prince. But their love is not permitted to develop further at this stage since Monime banishes Xipharès from her presence, thus providing Xipharès with a dilemma, for he has been given charge of Monime by his father. The next meeting between the young lovers occurs in Act IV, scene 2. Again what happens between Monime and Mithridate causes the dramatic nature of this scene, because Monime has fallen into Mithridate's trap, inadvertently exposing Xipharès to danger by revealing him as the real object of her affection. As in the case of the two previous encounters, an explanation or a revelation takes place, this time Monime confessing her guilt at admitting to the king that she loves Xipharès.

This analysis brings to light two important aspects of Racine's dramatic strategy. First, such a configuration of dramatic movement from one set of characters to another allows Racine to space his effects throughout the play. In other words, Xipharès and Monime do not declare their love for each other in the same scene. After Xipharès's declaration of love to Monime, we must wait until Act II, scene 1 for the clarification of her position, and Act II, scene 6 before

Monime declares herself to Xipharès. Act III develops the
action further, Racine thus delaying the reintroduction of the
pair of lovers until Act IV, scene 2. Their last scene together
is appropriately the last scene of the play. The confrontations
between Mithridate and Monime are similarly spaced (II,4;
III,5; IV,4 and the final scene). Once again, therefore, Act V
is dramatically problematic since it contains no scene of
major confrontation until Mithridate returns from the battle
in the company of Xipharès.

Secondly, the economy of repetition in the Racinian
confrontation requires that its principal quality, if each confrontation between major characters is to be effective, must
lie in its consequentiality. Consequences may not be explicit
either during or immediately following the relevant scene.
These emerge at times only subsequently. Xipharès's declaration of love to Monime provides us with a good example,
since it assumes significance only after Mithridate's return.
Equally, Monime's banishment of Xipharès at the end of Act
II leaves Xipharès's solution completely open, but there is no
doubt that it projects the action forward on the level of
expectation. In general, the consequences of the sort of
encounters I am discussing are immediately clear. Monime's
declaration of love for Xipharès will affect her relationship
with Mithridate, and her act of defiance in Act IV, scene 4
can only incite the revenge of the king.

Drama, especially tragedy, does not, however, consist
exclusively of our intellectual perception of the forward
movement of the action. Emotional response is certainly in
part a function of expectation and suspense. It is also related
to the progression of the action in that our response to a
particular type of situation, if repeated, may exhaust itself.
More importantly, emotional involvement possesses two elements crucial to the argument that follows: first, a quality of
immediacy, where we feel for the characters in the moment
they appear before us; secondly, the manner in which this
quality of immediacy combines with emphasis on the forward
movement of the action. At times it is even possible for these
two elements to be in competition with each other. Such a
cleavage within the temporal nature of response may be

demonstrated by turning our attention to a major feature of seventeenth-century tragedy, the *pathétique.*

The *pathétique* may generally be defined as that which arouses feelings of strong emotion, as that which is intensely moving, and is normally associated with suffering. In the seventeenth century it may be a device of staging, such as a prison, or it can be a structural device where characters meet at certain crucial stages of the action. The *pathétique* sometimes turns out to be an element in addition to the progress of the action, where the playwright invites the spectator to indulge in the experience of emotion for its own sake. In this sense the *pathétique* may be considered detrimental to the progression of the action. A suitable illustration of this would be Sabine in Corneille's *Horace.*

In *Mithridate* there are four examples of the *pathétique* I should like to examine, Act II, scene 6; Act III, scene 5; Act IV, scene 2 and the whole of Act V. All, except the second half of Act V, have Monime as the major source of the *pathétique.* In Act II, scene 6, the emotional involvement of the spectator derives essentially from the situation the characters find themselves in, but also from the way in which that situation will evolve; Monime declares her love for Xipharès after Mithridate has returned, but at the same time forbids Xipharès to approach her. Thus there is an immediate emotional effect, for we are happy that Xipharès's love for Monime should be requited, but the action is also advanced since Xipharès must now discover a means to evade his father's command that he be responsible for Monime.

In Act III, scene 5, the *pathétique* derives in part from the development of the action within the scene. Monime is confronted by Mithridate in circumstances of extreme pressure; he has already accused her of loving Pharnace, a charge he continues to make in the course of the scene. An additional element from our point of view is our knowledge that Mithridate has planned to set a trap for Monime. Our emotional involvement is immediate in our appreciation of her dilemma; is it in fact safe to confess her love for Xipharès? Our response is further heightened by her belief in Mithridate's sincerity and her subsequent revelation. But, crucially, the excitation of emotion is also relevant in a forward moving sense in that she has now placed herself and Xipharès in some jeopardy.

The case of the *pathétique* in Act IV, scene 2 is slightly different. The situation has certainly created an atmosphere of intense feeling: it is, of course, a continuation of events in Act III, scene 5. Monime must confront Xipharès and reveal that she is responsible for disclosing their secret. Here, however, any forward dramatic impulsion is absent. The way is soon cleared, once Monime has admitted her guilt, for a more immediate form of emotional indulgence. The characters lament their situation. Act IV, scene 2 in fact marks a dramatic impasse in the relationship of Monime and Xipharès, thus producing a certain stasis in the action, at least as far as they are concerned as a pair.

A similar weakness is apparent in Act V where almost no forward progression of the relationships between the characters is possible until the *coup de théâtre* of Mithridate's act of forgiveness in the final scene. It could be argued that recourse to a *coup de théâtre* is in some way related to the playwright's exhaustion of other types of dramatic variety. Act V concentrates first on Monime who laments her position both before and after the delivery of the poison, and then, from Act V, scene 4 to the end, on an emotionally charged description of the king's defeat and Xipharès's triumph. Thus the element of the *pathétique* does not arrest the action when our emotional involvement results at least in part from the action being projected forwards. The action is arrested rather when the *pathétique* invites only sympathy for the victim. Emotion in this case does not so much derive from the situation as become the situation itself.

All the preceding remarks about the progression in the action and about the avoidance of monotony in the dramatic effect of the play converge in some way in the notion of crisis, held to be so characteristic of Racinian tragedy. But the notion of crisis differs from play to play in the way that it is organised and prepared. This will be obvious if we compare, for example, *Andromaque* with *Mithridate*.

In *Andromaque* Oreste precipitates the crisis of the tragedy by delivering his ultimatum in the second scene of the play, an ultimatum whose implications are perfectly clear. They are so because in any case all the elements necessary to the development of the situation exist: Andromaque's refusal of Pyrrhus's love, Pyrrhus's constant fluctuations between Andromaque and Hermione, Hermione's growing sense of rejection, but at the same time her reluctance to leave Epirus. In certain other tragedies too the crisis is apparent from the very beginning of the action, the whole play comprising thereafter an exemplification of that crisis.

Such is not quite the case with *Mithridate*. Certainly, as we learn in Act I, scene 1, a momentous event has taken place: Mithridate has been defeated and is reported dead. This in itself is not a crisis, although the rivalry between Xipharès, politically faithful to his father, and Pharnace, a friend of Mithridate's Roman enemies, is now brought to light. Their political rivalry is compounded by their rivalry for Monime, the latter having been chosen by Mithridate as his queen two years before. Indeed Xipharès is about to declare himself to Monime, as he does in Act I, scene 2. What is dramatically important at this stage is that Xipharès and Pharnace feel free to speak about their love, Pharnace having already declared himself to Monime. But the choice facing Monime is never really presented as a crisis, since no dire consequences will ensue from her refusal to marry either son. On the other hand, Andromaque's refusal to marry Pyrrhus affects directly the life of Astyanax, even before Oreste's arrival in Epirus. It is rather the news of Mithridate's return in Act I, scene 4 which precipitates the real crisis of the play. Only at this point does the urgency of the action assert itself. In *Mithridate,* then, the spectator is a witness to the inception of the crisis and Racine allows us to observe the characters' growing perception of the crisis as it makes its impact upon them.

Moreover, the nature of the crisis does not remain static throughout the play. The crisis can be defined in one sense as Mithridate's potential discovery of the events that have taken place or been reported in Act I. But, at the same time, it can be defined as the exposure of Xipharès and Monime, in which case the play comprises two parallel but related crises. It is also possible to argue that the play constantly generates crisis as each character must contend with the problems he or she faces.

This leads in turn to another variation in the presentation of the dramatic action which could be termed the variety of optic. Not only is the characters' perception of events not the same in each case, but the characters are obliged to react to changes in the situation caused by others. Indeed Racine's plays often present themselves as a set of revelations in their turn requiring assessment and reassessment. Mithridate himself, for example, needs to readjust his apprehension of events at least three times during the play: first, when he believes falsely that Monime loves Pharnace; next, when he discovers that Monime in fact loves Xipharès; finally, at the very end of the play, following Xipharès's success against the invading Romans.

Monime too reassesses her position at crucial stages of the action, for example, after Mithridate's return (this is true of all the characters of course) and when Mithridate misidentifies the one she truly loves. In this regard, Act IV, scene 4 is certainly her finest moment, since it leads Mithridate to reconsider, albeit briefly, his plan of revenge. Lastly, Xipharès needs to find a means of avoiding Monime once she has banished him from her presence. One character's solution (in this case Monime's) becomes another character's crisis. The skill of the playwright thus lies in part in the degrees of subtlety characters bring to the evaluation of their circumstances.

At many points in this chapter I have freely used the term 'action'. The concept of action in Racinian tragedy appears to be problematical. Racine bears in part the responsibility for this given his own account of the art of tragedy. In his preface to *Bérénice,* he writes that 'toute l'invention consiste à faire quelque chose de rien', arguing in the preface to *Britannicus* that a tragedy should consist of 'une action simple, chargée de peu de matière'. A common complaint, especially of English-speaking audiences, is that in Racine's tragedies nothing ever happens, a view compounded to my mind by the description of Racinian tragedy as 'psychological'. David Maland's view is that the interest of Racine's plays lies less in the characters' actions but in their thoughts and emotions (*13,* p. 268). A first response to such a narrow and misleading conception is that the characters tell us things they have never before formulated in public, a form of action I shall explore in chapter 3. Another is that their conduct has important, and in some cases deadly, consequences for others. The latter are therefore acted upon in some way. We need, then, to redefine our understanding particularly of the notion of 'event' and to reach some conclusion, however tentative, about action in Racinian tragedy.

Certainly Racine's tragedies include a category of external events which bring, so to speak, the outside on to the stage, and which are clearly marked in time. In *Mithridate,* we witness Mithridate's return from the various perils he has endured after his defeat at the hands of the Romans, the arrival of the Roman army reported in Act IV, scene 7, Arbate's intervention in Act V, scene 3, following Arcas's delivery of the poison, both incidents dependent on an order from the battlefield, and finally Mithridate's last entrance. Other categories of event too, less spectacular but thematically no less important, figure prominently in the action. These are events relating to revelation and discovery. In Acts I, scenes 1-2, and II, scenes 1 and 6 Racine presents us with revelations of love made public for the first time, and in Act III with the discovery by the king of Xipharès's treacherous love for Monime; later Monime herself learns of Mithridate's deceit. The categorisation of such revelations as events seems all the more appropriate for the perilous consequences arising from them. Furthermore they act as temporal markers in the progress of the action.

Indeed discovery can at different times be the unveiling of factors external to the self, such as I have just described, and the fact of self-discovery, that is to say where a character is apprised of a completely new fact of self-knowledge. In *Mithridate* the following words of the king constitute just such an act of recognition:

Ah! qu'il eût mieux valu, plus sage et plus heureux,
Et repoussant les traits d'un amour dangereux,
Ne pas laisser remplir d'ardeurs empoisonnées
Un cœur déjà glacé par le froid des années!  (1417-20)

An event may consequently be defined as a perception on
the part of a character, or as an act of revelation to another
character, which represents a qualitative change in the course
of the drama. Action, then, represents what is irreversible,
that beyond which things cannot revert to their previous
state. Once Xipharès and Monime have declared their love
for each other, the previous order is overthrown. Monime's
realisation that she can no longer contemplate marriage to
Mithridate (IV,2) completely negates the direction of the
action up to that point (Xipharès has been urging her to
obey). This realisation is then acted upon in Act IV, scene 4.
Action is what moves us to a new order, in our case,
Mithridate's reconciliation with Xipharès and Monime,
events of all sorts acting as punctuation in that transformation.

# 2

# Structure and Meaning

THE distinction I have drawn between structure and effect on the one hand, and structure and meaning on the other is an artificial method of enabling us to understand how *Mithridate* exploits the sensibilities of the spectator at what I have called the primary level of response. But tragedy promotes its effects not simply for their own sake. Such sensationalism is the proper and legitimate domain of the melodrama. Effects in tragedy are generative of meaning, that is to say that the structure of a tragedy becomes part of the tragic meaning itself. Form therefore provides a way of seeing, a way of embodying significance. Form in this sense is interpretation. I now propose to examine certain aspects of the structure of *Mithridate* which, in themselves, stand for the view Racine offers us of the human condition.

One obvious relationship of structure to meaning is established by the use of irony, of which there are several categories: visual irony (rare in Racinian tragedy), verbal irony and that form of situational irony in plays we call dramatic irony. Dramatic irony in fact generates a synthesis between the verbal and the situational ironies. Dramatic irony serves therefore a variety of functions: it may increase the emotional impact of a scene where the spectator possesses knowledge of which a character or characters are deprived; it throws into relief more than one possible meaning of an utterance or of a situation; it may provide a contrast between two features of a character whereby one comes to negate the other. In addition to commenting on the modifications of meaning contained in the notion of irony which we shall see in certain examples from *Mithridate,* I shall also show how irony embodies in itself a comment on the tragic situation.

An important feature of irony is the disparity of knowledge between one character and another, or between the
characters and the audience. At a fundamental level, our
interpretation of the dramatic situation as spectators is affect-
ed and determined by our knowledge that a double meaning
attaches to individual utterances at crucial stages of the play,
and that one of these meanings escapes at least one of the
characters present. This may have consequences for the
dramatic action at any given moment. All these points
converge in the character of Mithridate himself.

Indeed a substantial proportion of the structure of *Mithridate,* in that it affects the king, promotes irony to the degree
that from his return until the end of Act IV all utterance in
the play is ironical in some sense, since from the beginning of
Act II the tragedy focuses on the revelation of information to
Mithridate. In the first place, we know that Xipharès and
Pharnace have both declared themselves to Monime. Mithridate is unaware that Xipharès is a rival for Monime's affection because Arbate, while not hesitating to expose Pharnace,
omits to reveal certain details concerning Xipharès's conduct.
The extent to which Mithridate is henceforward placed in an
ironical position is exemplified in his expression of relief at
Xipharès's reported fidelity:

> Oui, je respire, Arbate, et ma joie est extrême.
> Je tremblais, je l'avoue, et pour un fils que j'aime,
> Et pour moi qui craignais de perdre un tel appui,
> Et d'avoir à combattre un rival tel que lui.   (511-14)

Indeed Arbate's attempt to protect Xipharès (and himself)
has far-reaching consequences, one of which is the development of Mithridate's misinterpretation of Monime's response
in Act II, scene 4. Of course, Mithridate's words in lines
585-94 have one meaning for him and another for Monime.
Mithridate is referring to Pharnace ('un fils infidèle'), since
this is what Arbate has led him to expect. Monime, once
Mithridate has mentioned Xipharès at the end of the speech,
believes that the rest refers to him also. When Mithridate
calls for Xipharès, Monime reveals her anxiety for him, an

exclamation which is itself misunderstood by the king. In these circumstances there could be no more direct ironical reference to previous events, particularly the love of Xipharès and Monime for each other, than Mithridate's outburst:

> Xipharès n'a point trahi son père.
> Vous vous pressez en vain de le désavouer;
> Et ma tendre amitié ne peut que s'en louer.
> Ma honte en serait moindre, ainsi que votre crime,
> Si ce fils, en effet digne de votre estime,
> A quelque amour encore avait pu vous forcer. (596-601)

Thus Arbate's suppression of information generates a sequence of events which escape his original intention. The irony of Mithridate's error is compounded by bringing Xipharès and Monime closer together by making the prince her guardian. Mithridate further informs Xipharès that Monime loves Pharnace, the latter situation being swiftly resolved in Act II, scene 6 by her clarification of her own love for Xipharès. Monime's banishment of Xipharès establishes a further opportunity for irony when Mithridate's project to march on Rome provides Xipharès with a possible means of escape from his dilemma. Knowing as we do, and as Mithridate still does not, the requited love of Xipharès and Monime, the true significance of Xipharès's only speech in this scene is especially poignant:

> Trop heureux d'avancer la fin de ma misère,
> J'irai...j'effacerai le crime de ma mère,
> Seigneur. Vous m'en voyez rougir à vos genoux;
> J'ai honte de me voir si peu digne de vous;
> Tout mon sang doit laver une tache si noire. (939-43)

We are aware of the existence of another 'tache noire' in the present rather than in history and the more immediate reason why Xipharès is unworthy of his father. The irony deriving from the original misunderstanding continues until the end of the scene.

The sort of situational irony described so far has allowed us to perceive irony in the making where the characters have

unconsciously created the irony. *Mithridate,* however, in-
cludes one instance of irony deriving from a deliberate
strategy on the part of a character. In Act III, scene 5,
Mithridate decides to discover once and for all the real object
of Monime's affections. As spectators we are privy to this
information and are able to interpret Mithridate's words
accordingly in the scene which follows. Their meaning is of
course taken to be different by Monime. Monime in fact
suspects Mithridate's tactic for a moment (1073-78) but
finally yields to pressure from the king, disclosing her love
for Xipharès. The depth of the irony of the situation is
apparent in the following lines:

> Mais enfin je vous crois, et je ne puis penser
> Qu'à feindre si longtemps vous puissiez vous forcer.
>                                               (1097-98)

Interestingly, in Act IV, scene 4, the relationship between
Monime and Mithridate is reversed. She now possesses the
knowledge that Mithridate has tricked her. The king is,
however, unaware that his deceit has been discovered, hence
the strength of the irony in Monime's question: 'Quoi?
Seigneur, vous m'auriez donc trompée?' (1284).

In some cases the situational problem which has given rise
to the irony can be resolved. In Act II, scene 6, Xipharès
quickly learns that Monime loves him and not Pharnace. The
irony in some circumstances is only apparent or temporary.
In others irony is not so easily removed. No knowledge or
change in perception can resolve it. This form of permanent,
irremovable irony is present in *Mithridate* in several ways.
Monime, however unwitting the impulse that led her to it,
will always bear the responsibility of betraying Xipharès to
the king, her feelings of guilt being such that she attempts to
hang herself with her diadem (1453-58). In Mithridate's case
even his discovery of the truth fails to resolve the irony
entirely, since it gives rise to yet another irony, namely that
the very son who is willing and able to assist in the struggle
against Roman imperialism has now turned into a dangerous
rival who must be eliminated.

Nothing moreover can alter the fact that he himself has brought about the turn of events which negates his own desires and expectations. Monime argues forcefully that he is the architect of his own downfall in respect of their relationship:

> Vous seul, Seigneur, vous seul, vous m'avez arrachée
> A cette obéissance où j'étais attachée;
> Et ce fatal amour dont j'avais triomphé,
> Ce feu que dans l'oubli je croyais étouffé,
> Dont la cause à jamais s'éloignait de ma vue,
> Vos détours l'ont surpris et m'en ont convaincue.  (1339-44)

By endeavouring to lead the action in one direction Mithridate has simply succeeded in doing the opposite.

Certainly, ironies of the type I have examined contribute greatly to the dramatic and emotional impact of the play at the primary level of response, especially in the context of the pressure of utterance after Mithridate's return. The actual placing of certain events in relation to others ensures a considerable measure of emotional response. But irony also constitutes an optic of perception which transcends mere emotion. It takes us beyond the realm of emotional involvement and foregrounds on a more intellectual level relationships between characters or between characters and events. Irony has a distancing effect.

More than this, inherent in a structure based on irony lies a comment on human beings and their ability to control their existence. Irony implies that characters find it impossible to escape or control certain aspects of their situation. In the end result the crisis controls the characters. Not that they become mere cyphers: rather, the truths that they themselves perceive remain only partial. It is the completeness of the tragic form in Racine, and the articulation of its structure, that provides a whole truth. Irony is a means of demonstrating that 'the co-existence of incongruities is a part of the structure of existence' (cit. S. Hynes, *The Pattern of Hardy's Poetry* in *19*, p. 22). It is the privilege of the spectator alone to know that.

The notion of control is central to the dramatic action of any tragedy. This is particularly true of non-Hellenic tragedy where divine intervention (not always for the good) gives way to a concentration on more human qualities. This change of emphasis, however, does not necessarily lead to a more authoritative or more assertive humanity, *pace* the somewhat exceptional nature of the Cornelian tragic world. Various features of the dramatic action I have already examined at length in chapter 1 offer confirmation of such a view.

It is possible to discuss the structure of Racinian tragedy (with the exception perhaps of *Andromaque* and *Britannicus*) as a combination of concealment and revelation. In the last chapter, these aspects of structure were directly related to the nature of the spectator's emotional response on the level of expectation and suspense. Here my principal concern is with the relation of revelations to the structure in terms of their meaning as the latter is generated by their place in the sequence of events (revelations of course being events in their own right). For revelations are rarely voluntary in Racinian tragedy and are provoked as a result of a sequence of events or as a consequence of certain events. The news of Mithridate's death encourages Xipharès to tell Arbate of his love for Monime in Act I, scene 1, now that Pharnace is his only rival (35-36). His revelation to the princess (I,2) seems to be justified also by his enmity towards his brother (93-96), and by the suggestion that he wishes to save Monime from possible orders for her to be put to death (85-89). Monime confesses her love to Xipharès after Mithridate has accused her, in Xipharès's presence, of loving Pharnace, and is further tricked into revealing her love for Xipharès to Mithridate in III,5. The nature of the progress of the action as a sequence of provocations seems once again to underline the extent to which the characters are subject to, or prisoners of, the combination of circumstances to which they all contribute. Events therefore possess a significance beyond the characters' apprehension of them at the time of their occurrence, a significance which is determined by the place of those events in the structure of the tragedy. The play's meaning lies not so much in what each character says or does on an individual level, but in how they all combine unwittingly to create actually or potentially disastrous situations. The play's structure is the permanent embodiment of that meaning.

The structure of delay, another aspect of the dramatic action examined earlier, serves also to contribute to the elucidation of meaning, this time more explicitly at the level of character, particularly in the case of Mithridate. Mithridate has eventually to discover that Xipharès, Monime and Pharnace have all betrayed him in some way. Of course, reasons deriving from considerations of response can be adduced for deferring the disclosure of events to the king; it allows, for example, for the exploitation of certain emotional effects. But delay is equally significant for our view of the characters and of the action in general. The misunderstanding, vital to the progress of the action, by prolonging the process of Mithridate's comprehension of what is taking or has taken place, demonstrates another aspect of the control of the crisis. The error, and the length of time it takes to correct it, suggest the vulnerability of a king once so ruthless in his dealings with his family and with others.

Especially significant for the relation of structure to meaning is that his error in interpreting Monime's position *precedes* the exposition of his grandiose scheme for marching on Rome. Clearly, Mithridate's idea is militarily unrealisable, in the way that he presents it, for many reasons. The true obstacle to the realisation of such a plan is the extent to which he is under siege in his own kingdom as a direct result of the actions of his own sons and of Monime's declared love for Xipharès. His belief that he is in charge of his own situation is illusory, a fact underlined by the very structure of the play. The delay in securing confirmation of the actual course of events that have occurred in his absence until *after* he has announced his plan of conquest to his sons, increases the bitterness of the blow: in Act III, scene 4 the full nature of his position dawns on him:

> Quoi? de quelque côté que je tourne la vue,
> La foi de tous les cœurs est pour moi disparue?
> Tout m'abandonne ailleurs? tout me trahit ici?
> Pharnace, amis, maîtresse; et toi, mon fils, aussi?   (1011-14)

Moreover, even when Mithridate discovers the truth, events deprive him immediately of the opportunity to regain control over the situation. The reassertion of the power which his new-found knowledge might have provided him with is first of all negated by Monime's act of defiance in Act IV, scene 4, which leads to the self-doubting soliloquy of Act IV, scene 5. In this he recognises the folly of love so late in life (1417-20), but self-discovery arrives too late. Mithridate's dilemma is further complicated by the news of Pharnace's revolt and the arrival of the Roman army. His discovery and self-discovery thus coincide with the disappearance of any semblance of control he might have had over the action. The prolongation of his process of discovery and the rapid succession of events in Act IV not only increase the impact of the truth but also exemplify Mithridate's personal and military decline by his inability to apprehend the truth and impose his authority on his own situation.

*Mithridate,* however, does not end on a permanently catastrophic note. Racine allows a positive resolution to the love of Xipharès for Monime, and this resolution could be held to come from the king himself. One must, in these circumstances, ask whether Mithridate in fact succeeds in reasserting control after all. In some ways this is true (although in others, explored in more detail in chapter 5, it is not). Mithridate exacts his revenge on Monime by ordering her to take the poison, although he rescinds this order a little later. Eventually he blesses the marriage of Monime to Xipharès. On the other hand, Xipharès's courage has been a persuasive factor in his decision. Furthermore the defeat of the Romans, as he recognises, is only temporary (1681-82). Ultimately, however, Mithridate can only regain control of the situation by bequeathing it to his son at the moment of death. This could be interpreted, therefore, as his final defeat, this time at the hands of youth. Xipharès's survival is necessary for the continuation of the struggle against the Romans, and this survival is contingent upon sparing the life of Monime. It is in any case fitting that a structure based on revelation and self-discovery should end with such a recognition.

# 3

# Speech and Action

I N the preceding pages it has become obvious that language itself is a form of action through revelation and that revelation constitutes an event. Indeed, in a very fundamental sense, Racinian tragedy is a drama of language. It is dramatic less for its account of human motivation, character or passion, than for the way Racine invests with tragic implications the very act of speaking. Racinian tragedy is, as Roland Barthes calls *Phèdre,* a drama of 'accouchement'. Moreover, defining speech as a form of action enables us to develop further our understanding of the nature of the Racinian crisis and the pressures that accompany it. All utterance under these conditions creates a level of expectancy which depends on the requirement of the characters to say certain things. Whether or not they actually say them can have the most terrible consequences for their own lives and for that of others. That the characters meet on so few occasions, when often urgent explanations must be given, can only enhance the crisis of speech.

On the other hand, speech in itself can precipitate crisis. The false report of the king's death brings pressure on Xipharès not only to defend his own share of Mithridate's kingdoms, but also to protect Monime both from whatever secret orders for her death the king may have made (85-89) and from Pharnace's advances (93-97). This induces him to declare his love for her, first to Arbate, then to Monime. His declaration places him in a precarious position upon Mithridate's return to Nymphée because he is now an avowed rival to his father in love. The revelation of his love must then be kept from the king. Speech is therefore at the very root of conflict rather than just providing an account of it. It is rather

Monime's failure to respond adequately to Mithridate in Act II, scene 4 that plunges her into crisis, as we shall see more fully later. In these circumstances all utterance in the tragedy represents a danger to the characters, not only in what has already been revealed, but in what remains to be revealed. Contained in the act of speech is the fear of consequences for oneself and for others. Every speech, therefore, embodies the tension of the tragic action as a whole.

That there is something to be revealed implies that there is something unknown. In Racinian tragedy what is unknown is usually the result of things being hidden or suppressed. In *Mithridate* Racine underlines this aspect of the tragic action by the frequent occurrence of 'secret' in the text. Xipharès acknowledges the importance of his disclosure to Arbate by such a reference: 'Voilà tous les secrets que je voulais t'apprendre' (107). Mithridate too describes his project to march on Rome as his 'secret' (756). Alluding to his clandestine alliance with the Romans, which Xipharès and Monime are indeed aware of, Pharnace remarks: 'Vous savez mon secret' (368). Equally, Pharnace accuses Monime of being less than honest with him when she refuses to accompany him to his own territory:

> De mes intentions je pourrais vous instruire,
> Et je sais les raisons que j'aurais à vous dire,
> Si laissant en effet les vains déguisements,
> Vous m'aviez expliqué vos secrets sentiments. (283-86)

A final example occurs again in a speech of Pharnace when he betrays Xipharès to Mithridate:

> Mais Xipharès, Seigneur, ne vous a pas tout dit.
> C'est le moindre secret qu'il pouvait vous apprendre.
> (994-95)

The prominence of 'secret' is paralleled by the frequent occurrence of 'cacher' and the words and expressions associated with it. The significance of the theme is established in Act I when Pharnace suspects that Monime has something to

hide: 'Je crois voir l'intérêt que vous voulez celer' (289). It is
appropriate that Xipharès should then confess to his total
ignorance of Monime's 'sentiments cachés' (318), which is at
this stage true. Lastly, Mithridate speaks of his 'tendresse
cachée' for Xipharès (468). In this perspective, it is impossible to disregard such seemingly conventional interjections as
that of Xipharès: 'je ne le cèle pas' (82). In view of Racine's
economy of language, which incidentally reflects perfectly
the economy of time, there are no innocent expressions.

But if speech is revelation, revelation for each character in
the instant that it is made does not so much emerge as erupt,
thus reinforcing the urgency of the tragic crisis and the power
of the characters' feelings. Xipharès complains to Monime
that in the past 'Tout mon amour alors ne put pas éclater'
(198), whereas now things have changed: 'Mais enfin, à mon
tour, je prétends éclater' (98). Mithridate expresses himself
similarly at the unveiling of his plan in Act III, scene 1: '...il
faut que mon secret éclate' (756). All the meanings of 'éclater'
converge in the Racinian context. Speech bursts upon the
world, often quite violently; it shatters and fragments if not
always the self, then certainly those who are the object of
speech. In any case, in Racine's tragedies speech breaks
through a barrier which has hitherto remained uncrossed.

At least Xipharès's declaration in Act I, scene 2 is on this
occasion voluntary. This docs not always turn out to be the
case, as I observed in the context of the relation of revelation
to structure. Revelation is often provoked. Disclosure is
involuntary. Speech thus erupts as a result of extreme situations. Mithridate's misunderstanding of Monime's relationship with Pharnace and Xipharès's obvious distress at the
news impels Monime to speak out: 'Oui, Prince, il n'est plus
temps de le dissimuler' (674).

One particular danger of speech occurring as a consequence of provocation resides in the possibility of self-
betrayal. That characters abruptly remind themselves of their
susceptibility in this respect is often marked by a textual
indication of interrupted speech. *Mithridate* contains a
number of examples, two of which are particularly effective.
The first presents itself during Xipharès's declaration in

Act I, scene 2 after he has asked Monime whether in the past she ever took pity on his distress. Monime replies: 'Prince..., n'abusez point de l'état où je suis' (210), the punctuation suggesting that she has been on the point of revealing her love but has prevented herself from doing so at the last moment. Act III, scene 1 provides a rather similar illustration. Xipharès, in his response to Mithridate's grand military expedition, concentrates first on Pharnace's odious suggestion of an alliance with Rome and then on his own desire to fulfil his father's bellicose ambitions; but his words, towards the end of his speech, assume more and more a personal significance as he remembers his own misfortunes in love:

> Trop heureux d'avancer la fin de ma misère,
> J'irai...J'effacerai le crime de ma mère.  (939-40)

Speech obviously seems to have its own momentum in Racine's tragedies, a danger inherent in the very act of speaking. Indeed what precise limits can be set for what the characters say? Speech therefore involves a notion of restraint. On the occasion to which I have referred, Xipharès manages to retrieve the situation by evoking the memory of his mother's crime against his father, thus supplying an alternative explanation for his wretchedness. But the constraints the characters impose upon themselves are often visible only when they encounter difficulty in keeping to them. For there is sometimes a desire on the part of characters to indulge in speech, despite the perils that that may entail: Monime is unable to tear herself away from Xipharès, a situation she knows to be dangerous:

> Je me sens arrêter par un plaisir funeste.
> Plus je vous parle, et plus, trop faible que je suis,
> Je cherche à prolonger le péril que je fuis.  (740-42)

Indeed, the tendency to self-betrayal on the part of the characters is a condition of the act of deception Mithridate perpetrates against Monime, where he tests the limits of speech I have just referred to. The very essence of his trap is linguistic, both in the way he encourages her to reveal unwittingly what he seeks to know for certain ('Qui peut de son vainqueur mieux parler que l'ingrate', 1028), and in the way he conceals his meaning.

One conclusion that can be drawn from the provocation of speech is that all utterance in such circumstances is inopportune because the moment of speaking has not been chosen by the characters themselves. They are unable to control their own speech. This is as true of the listener (whom I shall return to in more detail) as to the speaker. Xipharès's declaration to Monime is unwelcome to the degree that it reactivates her love for him, as she confirms herself in Act II, scene 1, and creates difficulties for her in expressing her obedience to the king's wishes. But one of the most anguished comments on inopportune speech comes from Mithridate himself:

> Pourquoi chercher si loin un odieux époux?
> Avant que de partir, pourquoi vous taisiez-vous?
> Attendiez-vous, pour faire un aveu si funeste,
> Que le sort ennemi m'eût ravi tout le reste... (1301-1304)

Monime's refusal to marry Mithridate has exacerbated his already considerable misfortunes. It has already served to shatter his own confidence in ultimately defeating the Romans, especially as Monime's refusal immediately precedes the news of Pharnace's revolt and the Roman invasion.

But another form of provocation exists in the context of Racinian speech, which is the result of the dangers attendant upon the characters in encountering certain others and in the difficulty of avoiding the need to speak to them. Remaining silent is impossible. Speech is expected and obligatory. The tension is increased by the nature of what must be said. Racinian tragedy further magnifies this level of expectancy because of the infrequent occasions on which individual characters meet, and the development of the dramatic action arising from encounters involving different pairs of individual characters. Racine establishes therefore a direct relationship between the visual and the vocal. The playwright underlines this textually in *Mithridate* when, for example, the king declares that 'il faut que mon secret éclate *à votre vue*' (756).

The characters themselves are aware that seeing a particular character in itself comprises a form of provocation which will have certain consequences. As Monime explains to Phœdime:

> Phœdime, si je puis, je ne le verrai plus.
> Malgré tous les efforts que je pourrais me faire,
> Je verrais ses douleurs, je ne pourrais me taire.
> Il viendra, malgré moi, m'arracher cet aveu. (414-17)

Contained in this quotation is the involuntary nature of much tragic utterance. 'Arracher' also reminds us of the violent quality of speech in Racine. Monime stresses further the problems involved in certain types of encounter in her words to Xipharès in Act II, scene 6 which echo her previous remark:

> Je sais qu'en vous voyant, un tendre souvenir
> Peut m'arracher du cœur quelque indigne soupir. (729-30)

If speech can be provoked by a character's presence, it can only be avoided by enforced absence, by physical separation. Following the news of Mithridate's reappearance in Nymphée, Monime is understandably reluctant to meet him, for she knows that the state in which she must see him will make it difficult for her to pronounce what Mithridate expects. She first expresses her feelings in terms of hiding herself away (390). Finally, Monime announces that 'Je ne paraîtrai point dans l'état où je suis' (422). Similarly, she declares her intention not to appear before Xipharès in lines 414-17, where the connection between an encounter with the prince and involuntary confession is more obviously made. Hence the reason why she banishes Xipharès, as is evident from lines 729-30.

Concealing secrets, suppressing thoughts and feelings, and the need to avoid characters physically in order not to betray oneself in words points to the importance of silence in

Racinian tragedy. First of all, silence involves effort: it does not simply represent absence. Xipharès explains to Monime on the first occasion they meet in the play that:

> Jamais tous vos malheurs ne sauraient approcher
> Des maux que j'ai soufferts en le [= cet amour] voulant cacher.  (177-78)

Xipharès's efforts, it transpires, have been reciprocated by those of Monime, as she tells him in their second encounter:

> Hélas! si tu savais, pour garder le silence,
> Combien ce triste cœur s'est fait de violence!  (411-12)

Violence is present not only in speech but also in silence, as reflected in the opposition of 'étouffer' to 'éclater'. Once reasserted, Monime's love triumphs over her attempts to forget it: 'Ce feu que dans l'oubli je croyais étouffé' (1342).

If revelation is so important it is so precisely because it terminates silence. The characters themselves are acutely conscious of this aspect of speech. Xipharès exclaims to Arbate: 'Je l'aime, et ne veux plus m'en taire' (35). The characters reach a stage, therefore, where silence is no longer possible and can no longer be sustained. The violence of speech is a function of suppression:

> Cet amour s'est longtemps accru dans le silence.
> Que n'en puis-je à tes yeux marquer la violence...  (39-40)

All the themes I have examined so far concerning speech and silence converge in the speech in which Monime attests to her inability to suppress her feelings for a moment longer:

> Oui, Prince, il n'est plus temps de le dissimuler:
> Ma douleur pour se taire a trop de violence.
> Un rigoureux devoir me condamne au silence;
> Mais il faut bien enfin, malgré ses dures lois,
> Parler pour la première et la dernière fois.  (674-78)

The compulsive need to reveal and the harsh duty to suppress compete with each other; yet revelation triumphs. The use of 'enfin' suggests the limits of silence Monime has formerly imposed on herself. Those limits have now been transcended.

More significantly, Monime reveals the principal reason why speech assumes such importance for the characters and why speech is invested with a tragic quality. Certain things are being expressed for the very first time because the tragic crisis has provoked a situation of an unprecedented nature and of unprecedented proportions. These words have not been rehearsed. The skill of Racine as a playwright consists in conveying constantly the tension involved in formulating what has never been said and could never before be said.

Implicit in the words of Monime I have just quoted, however, is the desire for a return to a state of silence, for she is adamant that she is speaking of her love for Xipharès for the first and *last* time: 'Je vous le dis, Seigneur, pour ne plus vous le dire' (696). Monime explains to Mithridate too that she had intended that her love should revert to the status of a secret: 'Dans l'ombre du secret ce feu s'allait éteindre' (1335).

Indeed the very first act of the play announces the theme of a return to silence. After all, Mithridate's arrival in Nymphée requires precisely that, especially after Xipharès and Pharnace have declared themselves to Monime. An interesting distinction emerges, however, between Xipharès and Pharnace on the one hand, and Monime on the other. The brothers have spoken in Mithridate's absence. Monime declares her love for Xipharès to Phœdime and then to Xipharès *after* the king's return. In any case, the ability of the characters to control the action is again denied. An utterance, however innocent at the time of enunciation, reveals itself only subsequently as calamitous.

As with the emergence of speech, the return to silence is also violent:

> Il faut pourtant, il faut se faire violence;
> Et, sans perdre en adieux un reste de constance,
> Je fuis.  (743-45)

Monime thus expresses her need to wrench herself from Xipharès's presence and from the pleasure of conversing with him. The return to silence is, however, illusory, as Monime recognises after her involuntary confession to Mithridate:

> Les dieux qui m'inspiraient, et que j'ai mal suivis,
> M'ont fait taire trois fois par de secrets avis.
> J'ai dû continuer.   (1237-39)

This is particularly ironical in view of her earlier assertion to Xipharès that:

> Ma gloire me rappelle et m'entraîne à l'autel,
> Où je vais vous jurer un silence éternel.   (697-98)

The real drama of Racinian speech emerges here. Once things have been said, they cannot be unsaid. Secrets may remain hidden for a time, but once they are revealed, and the compulsion to reveal is at the centre of Racinian tragedy, they cannot be hidden again, at least not for long. Even the smallest compromise with silence is fatal. Monime, recounting her first encounter with Xipharès, informs Phœdime:

> ...mon cœur affermi
> N'a rien dit, ou du moins n'a parlé qu'à demi.   (409-10)

Monime, from her own point of view, has thereby begun to give some hint of her love. No retreat is possible once that process has begun. As she observes herself, 'Il fallait tout nier' (1134). Racinian speech, as it is exemplified in *Mithridate,* is dramatic because it is irreversible. Bringing secrets or secret thoughts into the open operates a qualitative change in the dramatic action. In this sense, all speech in Racine's tragedies is an event.

There are of course purely dramatic aspects to silence. It can be exploited as a production device, particularly where it is not explicitly marked in the text. Racine, however, sometimes provides indications of those points where silences should occur, as in Act II, scene 4, when the king observes to Monime:

Hé quoi? n'avez-vous rien, Madame, à me répondre?...
Vous demeurez muette... (579-81)

Silence, from a theatrical point of view, assumes great importance because each time characters meet we expect the silence to be broken. The empty stage is expected to be filled not only with people but with people talking. In fact, drama situates itself between the silence of the beginning and the silence of the end. The role of silence in Racinian tragedy thus evinces a very firm grasp of theatrical as well as of dramatic imperatives.

I have remarked earlier that silence is not simply absence. Silence is a space which is filled with things unsaid and unformulated. Silence is speech in potentiality, what Richard Parish calls 'silence signifying in spite of itself' (*22,* p. 396). Hence it can be 'read' or 'misread'. The silence indicated between line 579 and line 580 is a sign to Mithridate that Monime is unwilling to respond to him on any other level than that of obedience. It is also true that in another sense he has been given information which has led him to misinterpret Monime's silence. It is however worthy of note how Racine emphasises Monime's reluctance to speak by the line distribution in the scene; Monime is given seven lines out of a scene containing seventy-seven lines. Mithridate is able to interpret her silence because it 'speaks' for him: 'Je vous entends ici mieux que vous ne pensez' (586). However, just as Mithridate 'hears' Monime's silence, she also speaks in silence. As she remarks to Xipharès, while she was listening to his misfortunes, 'Mon cœur vous répondait tous vos mêmes discours' (690).

If, then, silence is a space filled with things unsaid, as Monime's encounter with Mithridate suggests, even within speech there can be silence. In this case silence represents that which is expected by one interlocutor but not at the same time enunciated. Speech contains an 'implied' silence. Hence, Monime's inability to respond adequately to Mithridate in Act II, scene 4 demonstrates that she acts out of duty not love, since her love is reserved for Xipharès. Her failure to say what Mithridate expects confirms to the spectator that, her love for Xipharès having been reactivated by his declaration, she finds it impossible to commit herself in the appropriate words to the king. Whatever she says to the father betrays what she has earlier declared to the son. Similarly, Xipharès in Act III, scene 1 refers to his need to leave Nymphée not because of Monime, but in order to expiate his mother's crime. The true meaning of the speech implies exclusion as well as inclusion.

More qualities of silence are illustrated in the first encounter between Monime and Mithridate. Silence can be provocative in the same way as speech to the extent that in Monime's case Mithridate is led into the misunderstanding which dominates the action in the middle section of the play. But Mithridate is all the more hurt by Monime's refusal to say what he wants to hear because silence can also constitute denial, as his outburst in lines 559-70 suggests. In Mithridate's eyes her reluctance to marry him implies a slight on his reputation as a great king and warrior (although Monime always voices admiration of his military qualities). Indeed, Monime's desperate situation at this point reveals another aspect of the tragic crisis in *Mithridate.* Characters find themselves in an inescapable dilemma, for they are trapped both by what they say and by what they do not say. If speech constitutes danger, then silence does not necessarily provide a means of escape.

In Chapter 1 the point was made that, if the few encounters between pairs of individual characters were to be effective, they should be consequential. The importance of consequentiality is reflected at the level of speech. The link between speech and what can result from it is well understood by Monime:

> Et quand de toi peut-être un père se défie,
> Que dis-je? quand peut-être il y va de ta vie,
> Je parle...   (1143-45)

The speech event entails moreover moral consequences. Monime realises that in revealing her love to Xipharès she has betrayed Mithridate, to whom she is betrothed. This is so even before speaking to Xipharès in Act II, scene 6. Speaking induces shame: 'Phœdime... Tu m'entends, et tu vois ma rougeur' (394). Indeed, all the time Monime is yielding to her love for Xipharès, she never loses sight of her profound moral sense:

> Je sais qu'en vous voyant, un tendre souvenir
> Peut m'arracher du cœur quelque *indigne* soupir.
> (729-30, my italics)

She perceives that Xipharès's presence would encourage her in her wrong-doing, a course of action she regards as unworthy of her. Only Xipharès's absence can spare her this indignity. So speech is not only an important aspect of the action in *Mithridate*: it also possesses its own moral dimension. For Monime, Pharnace and Xipharès speech involves guilt. By speaking in the way the brothers do to Monime they have become enemies of their father. Monime betrays the promise made to Mithridate by her own father and is guilty of betraying Xipharès. There is ultimately no comfort in speech or silence.

So far all my comments have primarily concerned the speaker. In performance classical tragedy certainly imposes a strain on the actor and actress. Speaking constitutes the obvious aspect of a performer's work. A less obvious but no less crucial feature of acting which must also command attention is listening. How, for example, is the non-speaker supposed to react, especially in the absence of stage directions? Interestingly, the Racinian text contains some indication that the playwright was aware of this aspect of theatre.

Characters in fact spend much of their time listening to others. In Act I, scene 3, for example, Xipharès does not speak until sixty-five lines into the scene. The most obvious illustration of the characters constituting an audience is Act III, scene 1, where Mithridate's first speech lasts for one hundred and eight lines. Tragedy, then, derives not only from what the characters say but from what they are obliged to hear. Racinian tragedy imposes a strain upon the listener, as indeed the constant references to 'entendre' and 'écouter' suggest.

Those who speak attest often to their awareness of the effect on the listener of what they say. If characters are disclosing thoughts and feelings of great moment, frequently for the very first time, the effect on the listener is held to be proportionate to the anxiety of the speaker. Xipharès tells Arbate: 'Je m'en vais t'étonner' (32). The reaction of astonishment is only appropriate since Xipharès will reveal himself to be a rival to his father's love for Monime to the *confident* of Mithridate himself. Xipharès indeed notes Arbate's reaction in the same scene, observing: 'Tu ne t'attendais pas, sans doute, à ce discours' (37).

The listener's reaction is naturally determined by the unexpected nature of the revelation. Xipharès is conscious of the impact his declaration of love has on Monime:

> Mais, avec quelque ennui que vous puissiez apprendre
> Cet amour criminel qui vient de vous surprendre...   (175-76)

Mithridate too watches his sons as they listen to his grandiose plan in Act III, scene 1: 'Ce dessein vous surprend' (787). Pharnace replies to his father: 'Seigneur, je ne vous puis déguiser ma surprise' (863). The relationship between 'entendre' and 'surprendre' is present in the verbal reactions of those who listen, where the word 'apprendre' can also be used to express surprise, as when Monime exclaims to Xipharès in Act II, scene 1: 'Ah! que m'apprenez-vous?' (191).

The juxtaposition of 'entendre' and 'surprendre' indicates how painful it is sometimes to listen, and the degree to which what is being enunciated is unwelcome or bewildering. An excellent example of this occurs in Act II, scene 6, the scene immediately following Mithridate's revelation to Xipharès that Monime is in love with Pharnace. Xipharès asks with some disquiet:

> Que dirai-je, Madame? Et comment dois-je entendre
> Cet ordre, ce discours que je ne puis comprendre?   (635-36)

Monime in her turn cannot countenance for a moment the erroneous connection made between herself and Pharnace: 'Pharnace? O ciel! Pharnace? Ah! qu'entends-je moi-même?' (640).The pain of listening is such that characters can only avoid it (as in the case of speech) by enforced absence. When Xipharès notes that Monime 'ne veut plus m'entendre' this is exactly analogous to her weakness and indulgence in speaking to him: hearing him speak is precisely what will in future be impossible and what in the present imperils their lives.

In some ways the circumstances in which characters are obliged to listen echo the violence that often characterises speech. Speech is forced upon the ears of the listener. In a rather paradoxical way, characters feel equally the compulsion to hear: hence the importance of commands referring to speech. The compulsive need to hear focuses particularly on Mithridate: he will after all be the principal listener in the play, given that events prior to his return must at some stage be revealed to him. His eagerness to learn why his sons have arrived in Nymphée at the same time is evident in his manner of speaking to Arbate:

> Parle. Quelque désir qui m'entraîne auprès d'elle,
> Il me faut de leurs cœurs rendre un compte fidèle.
> Qu'est-ce qui s'est passé? Qu'as-tu vu? Que sais-tu?
> Depuis quel temps, pourquoi, comment t'es-tu rendu?
>
> (479-82)

Or again:

> Parle, je te l'ordonne, et je veux tout apprendre. (503)

Similarly, Xipharès must discover Monime's feelings: 'On vient, Madame on vient... expliquez-vous, de grâce' (219). Indeed, the famous Racinian economy appears here not to be an abstract phenomenon or an external feature imported into the representation of an already tragic world. Economy itself is a part of the drama in that all Monime needs to say in order to satisfy him is 'Un mot' (220).

Act III, scene 4 contains the most imposing illustration of the need to know as it is expressed by the characters. Hearing things at second hand is not sufficient. The king cannot remain content with Pharnace's allegation that Xipharès 'ne vous a pas tout dit' (994). It is imperative that Mithridate see Monime but in order to *hear*:

> Qu'on appelle la Reine. Oui, sans aller plus loin,
> Je veux l'ouïr. (1025-26)

Just as meeting signifies speaking, so does it signify hearing.

The conditions of listening in fact include another version of silence, this time an 'active' silence. For while it is true that the listener does not speak, characters listen for what they expect to hear. Listening itself is an active phenomenon. It too constitutes participation in the action. Nowhere is this more pertinent than in Act III, scene 5 when Mithridate lays his trap for Monime: moreover, Pharnace has already told us of the king's vigilance in this respect:

> Le Roi, toujours fertile en dangereux détours,
> S'armera contre nous de nos moindres discours. (369-70)

Clearly Mithridate, in the speech in Act II, scene 4 beginning with line 551, pauses, awaiting an answer to his question, at which point Monime fails to say what Mithridate expects. This elicits from him the violent response leading to his accusation.

Interestingly, the spectator's own response to the meaning of the play is projected into the play itself because each character is confronted with the necessity of interpreting the words of his interlocutor. To this end, characters seek for clues, for indications of what others mean. Sometimes the character's search is unsuccessful, even anguished. Mithridate exclaims in Act III, scene 4: 'Qui m'en éclaircira? quels témoins? quel indice?...' (1023). On other occasions characters penetrate the real meaning behind what they hear. Mithridate knows very well the hidden sense of Pharnace's refusal to obey his father's command in Act III, scene 1: 'Tu

ne saurais partir, perfide, et je t'entends' (970). Similarly
Mithridate responds to Monime's attempts to evade the issue
in Act III, scene 5: 'Vous résistez en vain, et j'entends
votre fuite' (1095), thus providing a good example of what
J. L. Styan calls 'listening between the lines' (*33*, p. 53). In
this context, the ambiguity surrounding the word 'entendre'
('hear' and 'understand') assumes a crucial significance. 'Entendre' represents what should have been, rather than what
was actually, heard.

However, 'understanding'/'hearing' can also be 'misunderstanding'/'mishearing'. Mithridate's confidence in interpreting Monime is, in Act II, scene 5, based on a false premiss: 'Je
vous entends ici mieux que vous ne pensez' (586). As I have
already stated, one character's interpretation of another involves many difficulties, owing to its dependence in the first
instance on the accuracy of the information supplied. Mithridate has been misled by Arbate in Act II, scene 3 into
believing that only Pharnace has betrayed his father, even
though it is true that Xipharès has remained politically
faithful. It is thus possible for characters to lose control of
meaning, since what is necessary to establish the right meaning lies beyond their reach.

The proper interpretation of what characters say raises
another problem, how to judge the sincerity of others. As
Xipharès complains to Monime, 'Mais des fureurs du Roi
que puis-je enfin juger?' (654). What are the grounds for belief
in what one has heard? If belief depends on the fidelity of
information, Mithridate does not receive a 'compte fidèle' in
Act II, scene 3. The problem of belief finally imposes itself
on Mithridate in Act III, scenes 3-4. After Pharnace's outburst in which he throws suspicion on Xipharès, the latter
asks his father: 'Seigneur, le croirez-vous, qu'un dessein si
coupable...' (999). Mithridate responds initially by rejecting
all suspicion of his son. However, the king then confronts
directly the question whether he should or should not believe
Pharnace: 'Je ne le croirai point? Vain espoir qui me flatte!'
(1007). Belief poses more difficulties because Pharnace can
himself be suspected of harbouring a grudge against his
brother:

> Quelle faiblesse à moi d'en croire un furieux
> Qu'arme contre son frère un courroux envieux.  (1017-18)

But the refusal to believe is short-lived: no sooner has
Mithridate said, 'Non, ne l'en croyons point' (1021), than he
is seeking a means to confirm his non-belief. At this point he
calls for Monime in order to hear what she has to say.

Paradoxically, the confirmation of the information he
seeks can be achieved only by tricking Monime into believing
him when he offers her Xipharès in marriage. Speaking here
has a direct connection with 'feindre' and 'dissimuler' which
themselves relate to 'cacher' and 'secret'. Pharnace has already warned us of this possibility:

> Vous savez sa coutume, et sous quelles tendresses
> Sa haine sait cacher ses trompeuses adresses.  (371-72)

Moreover, Mithridate himself explains what conditions belief
and how this will assist him in his attempt to elicit the right
information from Monime, since 'L'amour avidement croit
tout ce qui le flatte' (1027). All this culminates in the irony
contained in Monime's lines:

> Mais enfin je vous crois, et je ne puis penser
> Qu'à feindre si longtemps vous puissiez vous forcer.
>                                                     (1097-98)

Why does Monime ultimately choose to believe Mithridate? The answer is in fact quite simple: because the speech
Mithridate makes here is precisely one that could be enunciated in other circumstances where deceit would be unneces-
sary. Mithridate's feelings about his son as expressed here
reflect the 'tendresse cachée' he alludes to earlier. By consciously feigning a position Mithridate in fact reveals a
sincere attitude, the attitude one might expect of a man who
loves his son. Even in a situation where the king consciously
'creates' and plays a credible role, he cannot control the
ultimate significance of his words.

While, then, speech as a form of action relates directly to
aspects of structure, particularly through the idea of revela-

tion and the notion of control, Racine invests the speech act, at the moment of utterance, with considerable dramatic and tragic qualities. Racine is highly aware of the immediate effect of speech and of the way in which characters are entrapped either by what they say or by what they fail to say. The public nature of theatre also underlines how the characters bring into the open, before an audience composed of other characters, their secrets and innermost thoughts. The situation then becomes irreversible. Speech represents a commitment, usually unwanted and unwelcome, and nearly always disastrous. This is not entirely so in *Mithridate* itself. But speech at the very least places the characters in dire peril. Above all, speech in Racine possesses an essentially theatrical dimension in exploiting the excitement and sense of expectation involved in the utterance. However unlikely it may seem at first sight, Racine's tragedies are the paradigm of theatre itself.

# 4

# Space and Time

THE concepts of space and time in seventeenth-century classical tragedy in France have been much misunderstood, since too frequently they have been considered in the light of authoritarian impositions rather than as constraints derived from purely aesthetic concerns. An appreciation of the latter has not always been helped by the turgid and often pedantic discussions of the dramatic theorists of the period. But on a close examination, even their writings manifest a desire for a dramatic experience which is direct and uncluttered. The spectator, if emotion is to be properly and fully experienced, must be taken to the heart of the matter with his mind free of the obstructions which can arise from the mental reconstruction of how characters move from one place to another and the need to relate the development of the characters to a broad expanse of time. Such a view may have its shortcomings, especially as a universal view of drama. But it has the virtue at least of emphasising a concentration of experience which seems peculiarly appropriate to the tragic genre. Indeed such concentration has always been considered as the major strength of Racinian tragedy.

Space and time in classical tragedy are therefore technical concerns serving as a framework for the action. They situate the spectator as well as the characters, creating a heightened form of expectancy. In theory at least, one place and no other suggests that a resolution to the tragic action forecloses the possibility of escape. A limitation on the time to be taken by the tragic action underlines the urgency of the characters' situations. Both constraints are productive of crisis.

But as many critics have demonstrated, space and time are also thematic entities, since the characters themselves have perceptions of their relation to the outside world, and perhaps more importantly, to history. In *Mithridate,* for example, the characters are aware of a geographical reality which at the same time contrasts with a geographical ideal. For this reason, we should beware, as critics, of over-determining the symbolic aspects of space in particular. To say, with Odette de Mourgues (in an otherwise highly suggestive chapter), that, 'In a way the place chosen has no real existence, in the ordinary meaning of the word, but only an ideal, symbolic existence' (*18,* p. 24) is to deny one important distinction made by the characters from their own individual perspective.

Let us begin, then, with the geographical 'reality' of *Mithridate* as enunciated by the participants in the tragedy. It is a place where certain events take place, the most recent being the defeat of Mithridate by the Romans in the region of the Euphrates (3). The climatic reality of the region in which the play is set is mentioned, being described by Mithridate as 'ces déserts' (762). But it is above all a space through which the characters have moved. Xipharès, for example, accounts for his movements to Arbate, describing how he had intended to rejoin his father at the eventual place of defeat but was diverted by the news of the king's death; thinking of Monime he has come instead to Nymphée (79-89). Mithridate too recounts how, following the battle, he managed, after much wandering, to rejoin his scattered army (451-54).

The breadth of Mithridate's knowledge of the territories surrounding Nymphée comes from having reigned over it for a period of forty years. Announcing his expedition to Rome he himself refers to the great familiarity he has with his lands (793). He has indeed held the balance of power in his part of the world and 'vengeait de tous les rois la querelle commune' (11-12). According to Xipharès,

> ...des rives de Pont aux rives du Bosphore
> Tout reconnut mon père;... (76-77)

Mithridate's sphere of influence is therefore vast; it not only extends over the thirty states he rules personally, but tran-

scends the narrow confines of geography to no less than
'l'univers'.

The evidence therefore suggests that a vast familiar world
exists for the characters outwith the confines of the space
represented by the stage. They know that there are other
places to which they may go, the 'ailleurs' so often mentioned
in the text. Xipharès tells Monime that 'Pharnace ira, s'il
veut, se faire craindre ailleurs' (165), since Nymphée is
Xipharès's inheritance, not his brother's (113-16). Arbate has
already intimated that Pharnace 'ira jouir ailleurs des bontés
des Romains' (130). The 'outside' is a place to which Mithridate is constantly impelled: he explains to Monime: 'Ma
gloire loin d'ici, vous et moi nous appelle' (544). Characters
have also arrived in Nymphée from other places, indeed from
a known to a lesser known land, as in the case of Monime
(256-57).

The outside world is not simply a 'real' space in the
memory or in the mind of the characters. It has direct links
with the space represented by the stage. That the latter is
regarded as one part of a larger space is particularly underlined by Nymphée's status as a port. Pharnace has ships ready
to leave (240) and Mithridate has made preparations to take
Monime with him after their marriage. Ports are thus places
of arrival and departure. From the beginning of the play
messengers bring news of Mithridate's death (225) and the
king himself arrives in the course of Act I, scene 4. Finally
the Romans invade Nymphée towards the end of Act IV.

The world outside the stage is not the only place to
benefit from its situation as a real geographical space. Racine
provides the stage space itself, the scene of much coming and
going, with a certain topographical substance. The characters
constantly mention other places within a larger expanse and
the immediate environs of the stage space. While Racine's
scene-setting at the head of the play specifies only the city
('La scène est à Nymphée, port de mer sur la Bosphore
Cimmérien, dans la Taurique Chersonèse') one assumes that
the action takes place in Mithridate's palace. Mithridate,
having attempted suicide on the false news of Xipharès's
death, launches one last assault on the Romans: 'Du *palais*, à

ces mots il fait ouvrir les portes' (1580). Arbate refers to 'ce *rempart* contre lui [i.e. Pharnace] défendu' (126), and in Act III, scene 2 Mithridate orders Pharnace to be confined in a tower (990). Indeed Racine does not forget to describe Pharnace's escape (1425). Another place with some significance within the palace is the altar, although on many occasions 'autel' could be held to signify marriage or sacrifice. However, the altar can be considered as referring to an actual place on two occasions. The first occurs in Act I, scene 3 where Pharnace says to Monime:

> Prêts à vous recevoir, mes vaisseaux vous attendent,
> Et du pied de l'autel vous y pouvez monter...   (240-41)

The second is to be found in Act III, scene 5 when Monime explains that preparations for a sacrifice have been made for the marriage ceremony (1077-78).

As in the wider geographical expanse, the palace is a place the characters move in. They seek each other out, as for example in the case of Monime desiring to see Xipharès in Act I, scene 2. We learn that Phœdime has been following Monime to save her from herself (1453-59). Phœdime, on the other hand, is asked by Monime to go and discover what is preventing Xipharès from appearing before her (1127-28).

The idea of the existence of space outside but close to the stage space is strengthened by the implicit proximity of characters at certain given moments of the action. In Act II, scene 4 Mithridate orders that Xipharès be called (595) and indeed he arrives ten lines later. Similarly Mithridate summons Monime in Act III, scene 4, her arrival ensuing after nine lines. While it would be foolish to adopt an over-literal attitude to such examples, they do indicate that Racine conceives of an 'integral' space. Moreover, one may legitimately ask oneself to whom these orders are addressed. One feature of Racine's tragedies which seems to bely the notion of Racinian space as a 'huis clos' is the presence of guards who are attested to in two scenes of *Mithridate*: Act II, scene 2, where they leave at the end of the scene accompanied by Pharnace and Xipharès, and Act III, scene 2, on which occasion they are addressed directly and ordered to seize Pharnace whom they convey to his tower. The immediate environs of Nymphée represent then a populated space, especially on the return of Mithridate's army which is described as ready to embark once again in line 1273.

What enhances most especially the notion of what one might call 'contiguous space' (i.e. that space we do not see but whose existence nearby is referred to by the characters) is the simultaneous occurrence of events, one of which we witness on the stage, and the other we are told about as taking place elsewhere. Many such examples can be cited. In Act II, scene 1, Monime declines to go with the others to welcome Mithridate (375-76), whose arrival has been witnessed by Arbate in the course of Act I, scene 4. In Act IV, scene 1, we know that the king is at the shore supervising his soldiers' impending embarkation; later in the same act, Arbate relates that these same soldiers refuse to leave and that Pharnace and Xipharès are present at the mutiny. Lastly, Arbate in Act IV, scene 4 tells Monime that the king and Xipharès are on their way to the palace after repelling the Roman army.

In the preceding remarks I have tried to show how Racine provides a framework with regard to place which situates the characters in a world which for them possesses a certain reality at a primary level. My aim has been to locate the basis of that reality in the characters' minds. This reality can now be considered from the point of view of its dramatic quality and significance, in which movement plays an important part.

Nymphée as we have seen, is a place of coming and going where, however, certain arrivals and departures are endowed with more significance than others. *Mithridate,* along with *Phèdre,* is first and foremost a tragedy of return, whereas most other Racinian tragedies are dramas of arrival or departure. The king's return is calamitous for Pharnace and Xipharès, who have expressed feelings which should have remained suppressed and which now threaten to expose them as traitors. It also disrupts the ambitions and desires of certain characters. The king himself is well aware of the implications of his return to Nymphée, declaring it to be 'mon funeste retour' (523) and 'retour qui me tue' (391). Moreover, his escape from the battlefield near the Euphrates is blighted by a return not to security but to the discovery of 'des malheurs qui m'attendaient encore' (456). Indeed, it is almost as if Nymphée has a magnetic quality, since all the characters are to be found there at the same time and for the same reason, i.e. Monime. One return has more felicitous consequences, the return of Mithridate in Act V. It is also, however, the return of Xipharès, earlier condemned by his father and ordered to leave by Monime. This time Xipharès returns to her, not Mithridate. Rather the king returns her to his son who can claim to have loved Monime first, the full significance of which will be examined later.

Just as arrivals are dramatically charged, so are departures, which are nearly always urgent. Pharnace urges Monime that they should wait no longer to marry and 'il faut.../...presser notre départ' (237-38). No sooner has Mithridate returned from his place of defeat than he is ready to be on the move again:

> Et, sans perdre un moment pour ce noble dessein,
> Aujourd'hui votre époux, il faut partir demain.  (545-46)

In fact the contrast of mobility in other characters with the immobile Monime is quite marked. Just as Pharnace, Xipharès and the king gravitate towards her in the course of the action, so she repels Pharnace and eventually Mithridate, and commands Xipharès to abandon her. At the beginning of Act V, she is indeed left alone, only to be returned to again by Xipharès and his father. In this way, Racine seems to provide a point of emotional stability and strength in Monime. The dramatic action of *Mithridate* is therefore underpinned by patterns of movement from one place to another.

Nymphée and the surrounding territory also offer opportunities for the playwright to intensify the more profoundly thematic significance of certain aspects of space in *Mithridate*. Twice in the play characters refer to the unpleasant climate of the play's geographical setting. Pharnace attempts to seduce Monime away from 'ce climat sauvage', promising

her 'un ciel plus heureux' (227-30). Racine conveys the
future hostility of Mithridate and the general emotional
atmosphere of the action by highlighting the inhospitable
nature of the region: Monime complains to Phœdime that:

> ...m'arrachant du doux sein de la Grèce,
> Dans ce climat barbare on traîna ta maîtresse.   (1527-28)

Racine thereby suggests not only violence in the transfer from
one place to another ('arracher'), but also the existence of a
more ideal locality. Moreover, that Monime should find
herself betrothed to the king of 'ces déserts', as Mithridate
himself describes his territory, and now pursued by Pharnace,
assumes a greater irony since Nymphée was originally intended as a place of asylum for her (977). Mithridate despatched
her 'dans ces lieux éloignés de l'orage', therefore, only to be
confronted by an even greater peril.

Monime's dilemma in responding on the one hand to
Xipharès whom she loves, and rendering obedience to Mithridate whom she does not, is further emphasised by the ambiguity of the altar, a place of long-awaited fulfilment in
the king's marriage to Monime, especially after so many
misfortunes. It is obvious to Mithridate, however, that the
altar represents rather a place of sacrifice for Monime: 'Vous
n'allez à l'autel que comme une victime' (552).

The pleasant memory Monime has of her homeland
constitutes an alternative, now lost, to the unpleasant climate
of her present location. This ideality of space may also be
embodied in a construct which is entirely the creation of an
individual character. The principal example in *Mithridate* of
space representing an ideal is unquestionably the king's
projected expedition to Rome. Early in the play, the power of
space is the measure of Mithridate's status: the physical world
has been his only enemy, whereas all human opposition has
bowed to his commands (77-78). Now his position has
changed: 'Je fuis, ainsi le veut la fortune ennemie' (759). As
in the past, so now, Mithridate argues, he can resurrect his
fortunes.

But in the course of Mithridate's great speech which opens Act III, a subtle shift can be observed to take place from the realities of his situation, where all opposition to the Romans except his own has collapsed (781-84), to the manner in which he conceives of the progress of his long march, to which no obstacles are envisaged. The Black Sea will carry him to the Danube in two days, where an alliance with the Scythians will deliver him up the gates of Europe (797-800). His army will grow and the peoples he encounters will welcome him as a champion against tyranny (801-804). Others will follow him to Italy (805-12). Even Italy will rise, its conquest all the easier because the Roman legions are pursuing Mithridate elsewhere, and the Italians will accept the king as their leader (813-30). He ends this part of his speech with an exhortation to burn the Capitol, the potential scene of his own earlier humiliation (831-42). Mithridate thus moves from a realistic appraisal of his situation to no less than a reconstruction of space, from reality to ideal conquest, not only over the Romans, but over space itself.

While opposition to the Romans forms a key element of *Mithridate,* the power struggle also takes place within the king's own family. Nymphée itself and Mithridate's other kingdoms are symbols of power. The domains where one character has ascendancy over another are delineated from Act I, scene 1: Xipharès does not recognise Pharnace's power in Nymphée, that part of the Bosphorus belonging to Colchis, which has always been considered part of Xipharès's inheritance. Xipharès thereby legitimises his presence in Nymphée as opposed to Pharnace, who has come there for less respectable reasons.

Possession of a place implies furthermore the will and ability to rule, which Monime finds questionable in the case of Pharnace. How can he offer her his own lands when, as a secret ally of the Romans, he is not his own master (279-82)? Their potential power and ability to rule in their own right provides another element in the distinction Racine establishes between the two brothers. For this reason, perhaps, Pharnace is so eager to ally with his brother at the news of

Mithridate's return: 'Rendons-nous, vous et moi, maîtres de cette place' (360). He knows that his own power is limited.

If possession of space is so crucial, it follows that displacement is equally important. Arbate misinterprets Xipharès's attitude to the king's disappearance, thinking it to be 'l'ardeur de régner en sa place' (15), an assertion immediately denied by Xipharès. The subject later becomes an issue between Xipharès and his brother:

> Quoi? nous aurons d'un père entendu la disgrâce,
> Et lents à le venger, prompts à remplir sa place...   (295-96)

Such is, though, Pharnace's intention. In fact displacement of Mithridate extends in his case not only to territory but to Mithridate's place in Monime's life. Xipharès certainly interprets the situation in this way. Pharnace has, he remarks, already spoken to Monime 'et s'offrit en sa place' (96). Pharnace argues later that his inheritance of the kingdom of Pontus renders his claim to Monime entirely legitimate since she already bears its crown (235-36). Xipharès is eager to deny to Monime any similarity between his brother's intentions and his own:

> Ne croyez point pourtant que, semblable à Pharnace,
> Je vous serve aujourd'hui pour me mettre en sa place.
>                                                      (179-80)

The king himself suspects that his sons wish to rule in his stead. His suspicions are aroused by their very presence in Nymphée when they should have been protecting what had been entrusted to them (423-26). Mithridate's suspicions are repeated to Arbate in the following scene (475).

Characters, then, by occupying a space, impose their presence within it. But presence is not always necessary to convey a sense of power. This can also be achieved by a character who is absent. Even after the news of Mithridate's death in Act I, the characters show a constant awareness of a king whose sphere of influence is no less than the universe. Racine thereby enhances the king's stature by constant reminders of his power. His presence is inescapable in the wide geographical expanse of the eastern Mediterranean which is 'tout plein de ses exploits' (301), and which has seen him rise again at the moment he seems to have suffered his last defeat (769-70). He himself envisages the Romans expecting to find him in his own territories when in fact he plans to be elsewhere (829).

Two particular instances illustrate Mithridate's capacity to exercise power from afar. He had conveyed to Monime the diadem through the intermediary of Arbate, thus persuading her to undertake the journey from Greece to Nymphée (53-56). From that moment the diadem will perpetually remind Monime of Mithridate's control over her destiny (541-42). In addition, such is the power of Mithridate's voice that Xipharès imagines him accusing heaven and his sons for their failure to avenge him while he is lying unburied in his own land (299-306). Mithridate's power endures to the last when he sends Monime poison from the battlefield. No greater power of the king can be suggested than the way in which he seems to abolish distance.

On the other hand, Racine articulates in *Mithridate* a contraction of space which is rendered all the more effective for the evocation of the vast geographical expanse I have mentioned. This contraction reflects Mithridate's diminishing power, not only as a conqueror but also in his private relations with other characters. The contrast between the victorious and the defeated Mithridate is starkly portrayed. His former ubiquitousness is represented by his restlessness. Pharnace describes him as the enemy of rest (881), an idea the king conveys himself: 'Sortant de mes vaisseaux, il faut que j'y remonte' (1047). His kingdom has stretched from the Pontus to the Bosphorus. How the situation has now changed! He is:

> Vaincu, persécuté, sans secours, sans Etats,
> Errant de mers en mers, et moins roi que pirate,
> Conservant pour tous biens le nom de Mithridate... (562-64)

His kingdom, previously composed of thirty states, has now disintegrated into 'le débris [d'un malheureux empire]' (18). Pharnace eagerly awaits the Romans who are fast encroaching on his territory. Even Mithridate realises that the strength of the Romans is now such that their army cannot be defeated in the East (773-74). The final irony is that, just as he is preparing himself and his army to depart on his audacious venture, the Romans besiege Nymphée.

The contraction of space in *Mithridate* also entails consequences for the relationships between the characters. Previously their dispersal had resulted in the avoidance of conflict. That they are presently reunited in the same place can only end in the expression of feelings which would not otherwise have been enunciated. Now confrontation is inevitable. Moreover, contraction of space in real terms reflects the increasing isolation of the characters. Monime, before hearing of Xipharès's love, pleads for protection from him because she is 'Sans parents, sans amis, désolée et craintive' (135). It is Mithridate who expresses the feeling of isolation so bitterly. He has been betrayed first by Pharnace, then by Xipharès and finally by Monime, 'le seul bien qui me pût consoler' (1306), all of which culminates in his passionate outburst of lines 1013-14. Thus a king whose influence extended to the universe is reduced to an impotent figure in his own house. As Odette de Mourgues writes: 'the giant whose legs bestrode the ocean dies in sheltered and homely surroundings' (*18*, p. 28).

In the same way that Racine builds up a picture of 'real' geographical expanse, he is careful to provide a sound historical and temporal basis for the action of *Mithridate*. The expanse of space is more than matched by the expanse of time represented by the king's career of war and conquest. Several references are made to the forty years Mithridate has spent in his struggle against Roman imperialism (9, 879, 910), and to the fact that he has outlived the most important generals Rome could range against him (10). Other precise indications of time help equally to situate the action. Pharnace has been in Nymphée for eight days (483) and Mithridate has been absent for one year (435). Monime has spent 'deux ans d'ennuis' in Mithridate's kingdom (1173).

Moreover, Racine makes it quite clear that the diverse elements of the play's intrigue are of long standing, since on several occasions the characters employ the phrase 'dès longtemps' and similar expressions. For example, Pharnace's treachery and inclination for the Romans are not recent (25 and 516). Mithridate's choice of Xipharès as his heir apparent dates from long before the action of the play begins. This is equally true, and certainly more importantly so, of Xipharès's and Monime's love for each other, as they themselves recount its history (39 and 679-80), or as Pharnace reveals it to Mithridate (997).

In the cases I have just cited, the phrase 'dès longtemps' merely situates certain facts in time. Mithridate's use of the expression gives rise to a somewhat different implication when he says to Monime: 'Vous devez à ce jour dès longtemps vous attendre' (450). For Mithridate it signifies the sense of fulfilment he would like Monime to share. The expression in Mithridate's speech provides therefore an ironical temporal parallel both with the length of time Monime has loved Xipharès and her 'deux ans d'ennui' in Nymphée.

The more precisely thematic significance of time emerges on the level of the characters' discussion of the past. Indeed, the past cannot be separated from the present for it may directly determine the characters' actions or feelings. In Racinian tragedy the past is often a source of guilt, either potentially or in actuality. While with Xipharès guilt is rather by association – his own mother betrayed to the Romans the territory and treasure she was entrusted with (Pharnace is Mithridate's son by another wife) – his consciousness of the burden of this memory is expressed to Pharnace as another crime which can be imputed to him (363-64). The past is equally important to Monime on a personal level. One reason why she refuses Pharnace's offer of marriage is that her acceptance would constitute a betrayal of her father, killed by the Romans for his alliance with Mithridate (248-66). Time, then, is not something the characters can escape from any more than space. They are almost prisoners of it. It constitutes a burden in itself. The past, of course, also contains the present. There is no reason to believe that Mithridate on his return will be any different from what his previous actions imply. History thus acts as a precedent. The king has already had several mistresses put to death because of his jealousy (87-88), and has sacrificed two sons for suspicions aroused on another occasion (349-50).

But the burden of history in *Mithridate* is not as crushing as in other plays of Racine. *Mithridate* directs us in fact to a more positive future than in any other tragedy except perhaps *Alexandre*. Xipharès and Monime are, moreover, unique in that they survive as a couple with a fruitful life before them. *Mithridate* is alone in suggesting such a future, at least in suggesting a future that does not require atonement for the past. This is particularly so because the love of Xipharès and Monime is not a sin. Certainly they have committed a crime in disobeying Mithridate. But, as Xipharès pleads in his defence:

> Qu'il te suffise donc, pour me justifier,
> Que je vis, que j'aimai la reine le premier...   (45-46)

Xipharès develops this argument more fully in his declaration to Monime:

> Si le temps peut donner quelque droit légitime,
> Faut-il vous dire ici que le premier de tous
> Je vous vis, je formai le dessein d'être à vous...   (192-94)

Theirs is not a real betrayal (certainly not in the sense of Hippolyte's disobedience and Phèdre's betrayal of Thésée), their fundamental innocence being rewarded at the end of the play.

For Racinian characters, as I have remarked, the past is firmly included in the present. A contributory factor to this conflation of time is memory, another way in which the past is inescapable. Sometimes memories are pleasant, but more often than not they recall disagreeable states of being, as when Monime reminds Xipharès of his despair at the time of

Mithridate's offer of marriage to her. They are memories she
also shares (681-88). In *Mithridate* the characters' greatest
concern is sometimes not so much what they remember
themselves but what others may have forgotten. Xipharès
fears that Monime no longer recalls his grief at their farewell
(203-204). Mithridate accuses Monime of ingratitude in her
failure to recall how he has raised her above her origins, a
charge she indignantly refutes:

> Je n'ai point oublié quelle reconnaissance,
> Seigneur, m'a dû ranger sous votre obéissance.  (1323-24)

The king attempts to rekindle Monime's gratitude by evoking
an image of the past and by attempting to reimpose himself
on her memory: 'Revoyez-moi vainqueur, et partout redouté' (1294). Such a memory, however, has completely lost its
effect, especially after the re-emergence of Monime's love for
Xipharès.

Characters may indeed wish to efface certain memories
from their minds. Mithridate, albeit misrepresenting to himself Monime's relationship with Pharnace, exclaims: 'Je veux
laisser de vous jusqu'à votre mémoire' (1092). He reaches the
height of tyranny, however, in wishing to abolish Xipharès
from Monime's memory (1319-20).

But Racine's characters find it impossible to forget, however much they attempt to do so. After his mother's treachery, Xipharès 'forgot' his love for Monime. But no sooner
had he heard the news of Mithridate's death than the queen
'Avec tous ses attraits revint en ma pensée' (84). Mithridate's
desire to obliterate the memory of Monime's crime in loving
his son, is countered by Monime herself reminding him of the
past:

> Cependant, quand je veux oublier cet outrage,
> Et cacher à mon cœur cette funeste image,
> Vous osez à mes yeux rappeler le passé...  (1307-1309)

On the other hand the king has been responsible for thwart-
ing Monime's attempt to forget her love for Xipharès
(1341-44).

As the theme of memory suggests, time, as well as possessing an objective significance in terms of chronological situation, is an aspect of the characters' consciousness. Nowhere is this apprehension of time more obvious than in their realisation that decisions must be made which will determine their immediate circumstances, or in certain cases their lives. The compression of time and space activates what has been endured or remained latent over a long period of time. Suddenly urgency is required.

Time is therefore considered precious by the characters. No moments can be set aside for relaxation or leisurely deliberation. Moments not spent in deciding how to cope with the crisis are lost and irretrievable, the latter term representing perhaps one of the most important characteristics of Racinian tragedy. In Act I, scene 3, Pharnace presses Monime to hasten their departure (237-38). Mithridate's expedition must be undertaken without delay, 'sans perdre un moment' (545) and 'sans différer' (855). The perils of delay are expressed by Monime to Xipharès after the discovery of their mutual love:

> Allez: de ses fureurs songez à vous garder,
> Sans perdre ici le temps à me persuader... (1261-62)

In Act II, scene 6 Monime remarks upon how her pleasure in speaking to Xipharès is a danger to them both (740-42).

Indeed the tragic crisis marks an acceleration of time in the Racinian universe, where in the space of one day developments built up over many years reach their moment of climax. Moreover, so much is experienced in so short a time, as Monime herself perceives (641-44). The moment can expand to include a life-time's suffering: 'Combien en un moment heureux et misérable!' (712). The importance of a single day is enhanced by comparison with the longer period evoked in the course of the play. Xipharès is thus conscious of the implication of Pharnace's suggestion that Mithridate should throw himself upon the mercy of the Romans:

> ...O ciel! qu'osez-vous proposer?...
> Qu'il démente en un jour tout le cours de sa vie?   (906-908)

But even with this acceleration of time there is no panic in Racinian tragedy, but a heightened and unendurable aware- ness that the next moment may be the last. Developments which have been evolving 'dès longtemps' are perceived as having a term. At the very moment of speaking to Xipharès, Monime can speak of 'ce moment, le dernier qui nous reste' (739). The sort of finality present in all Racinian tragedy has various values, however. It can be used as a threat, as when Mithridate warns Monime about the inclination he thinks she has for Pharnace: 'Ou bien vous l'avez vu pour la dernière fois' (594). It can also represent a reality: Monime will speak to Xipharès 'pour la première et la dernière fois' (678). It is not important whether this is actually the case. What counts is that the characters think of each moment as if it were the last, as does Xipharès who believes his farewell to Monime in Act IV really to be 'pour toute ma vie' (1183).

What precisely makes this day so different from those that have preceded? It must be, as I have attempted to show at various stages of my discussion of aspects of *Mithridate*'s structure, that a qualitative change has occurred where no return to a previous order can be contemplated. Only in this sense is there a break with the past leading to an uncertain future. That characters recognise this 'rupture' is often con- veyed by the negative 'ne... plus'. The play begins with Xipharès's confession to Arbate of his love for Monime: 'Je l'aime et ne veux plus m'en taire' (35). Similarly, Monime explains that 'Il n'est plus temps de le dissimuler' (674). The characters' perception of a radical transformation in their position is amply demonstrated by the case of Mithridate. On his return he comments that Arbate sees him 'Non plus comme autrefois cet heureux Mithridate' (436), which he repeats to Monime (1041). The irretrievability of his past glory is all the more marked in his earlier appeal to her: 'Revoyez-moi vainqueur, et partout redouté' (1294). This is the last desperate cry of one who knows that the battle he might earlier have considered as an easy victory is lost.

Time and place, then, have a thematic significance tran- scending the confines of purely technical concerns. A combi- nation of circumstances, over which the characters are unable to impose their individual will, bring them together so that a solution to long-standing problems can be found, but always at a price. There is, however, no sense in *Mithridate* that superior forces conspire to bring this about. Few of Racine's plays, if any, can be considered tragedies of fate in the external sense of that term. *Mithridate* is certainly not one of them. Fate can however be used to describe an internal mechanism which, given the obsessions and passions of the characters, unfolds in a particular way. The seeds of the dramatic action have been sown long before, by the characters themselves, who could not have been aware of their future consequences, although retrospectively they become all too aware of them.

# 5

# Character and Action

CHARACTER is the most problematic aspect of drama. Characters are, after all, only words on a page: they have no existence beyond what those words tell us and we are permitted to speculate on their lives beyond the stage only if they themselves allude to it. The problem of character in Racinian tragedy is compounded by the description of the action as 'psychological'. In one sense the term is inescapable, for Racine's emphasis is on motivation and the operation of the passions. In another sense the term is misleading and unhelpful because it implies a description rather than an enactment.

From the point of view of drama, our major consideration must be the manner in which characters promote action. Characters in other words are not displayed for our inspection, the 'internal' workings of an individual character being in themselves insufficient to provide the action necessary to sustain a five-act tragedy. We are therefore concerned with the interaction between a number of characters. Most importantly, as I have constantly emphasised, the action thus generated is consequential. This is true even on an individual level. Racine's plays relate, as Odette de Mourgues rightly states, 'the fight between man and the passions which destroy him' (*18*, p. 82). But the characters' feelings will determine the action not only in terms of what happens to themselves but in terms of what happens to others. Equally, those others may have determining passions in their turn. The conflict which arises forms the action of the tragedy.

Conflict derives of necessity from difference and is reinforced by a sharp differentiation between the characters on the basis of their qualities, although this may not always be in terms of direct oppositions. Differentiation is important on two counts: the characters' evaluation of each other, correct or otherwise, determines in some measure their future actions; it also helps the spectator to structure his response to an individual character and to the action as a whole.

In *Mithridate* the qualities of the characters are such that little ambiguity exists in our attitude towards them. Xipharès, for example, is immediately identified as sympathetic by his display of faithfulness to his father and describes himself as 'plus que jamais à mon père fidèle' (27). His sense of devotion is longstanding; he has been 'dévoué dès l'enfance' (100). This is not simply a strategy designed to earn the support of Arbate in his ensuing rivalry with Pharnace. Xipharès is genuinely indignant in Act III, scene 1 at the very suggestion that his father should surrender to the Romans. His support and admiration for his father is at the same time an encomium and an exhortation to resist (906 seq.).

Xipharès's stature in the play is of course enhanced by inevitable comparison with his brother whom we know to be an ally of the Romans (22). Pharnace's villainous nature is confirmed by his behaviour with Monime in Act I, scene 3, where his brusque approach to the princess is in direct contrast to Xipharès's more polished and gentle speeches in the preceding scene. Here Xipharès's deferential attitude is beyond reproach. Xipharès is clearly identified as Monime's protector, especially as she displays more sympathy for him than for Pharnace. Xipharès is, moreover, keen to distinguish his own attitude from his brother's (179-80). Later in the scene with Pharnace and Monime, he confirms that he is the rightful heir to his father in the face of Pharnace's treachery (291 seq.). But, as I shall show in greater detail later, Xipharès also takes care to distinguish himself from his father, whose behaviour he has not always sanctioned. In Act I, scene 1, he describes how Mithridate's treatment of Monime in the early stages of their relationship fell far short of being honourable: instead of offering her marriage and 'des vœux dignes d'être écoutés':

> Il crut que, sans prétendre une plus haute gloire,
> Elle lui céderait une indigne victoire.   (51-52)

Above all Xipharès is singled out by Mithridate as a worthy son, 'ce fils si fidèle' (474). The king speaks of his 'tendre amitié' for Xipharès (598) who hates the Romans as much as he does (466). After reassurance from Arbate on his son's behaviour, Mithridate admits that 'Je tremblais...pour un fils que j'aime' (512), which finds an echo much later when we learn that at the false news of Xipharès's death during the battle Mithridate 'en a versé des larmes' (1563). That Mithridate experiences such emotions for his son is also recognised by other characters: Phœdime, comforting Monime after Mithridate's trickery, asks of the king: 'Voulait-il perdre un fils qu'il aime avec tendresse?' (1151). Given the way Racine has portrayed the characters' qualities, this is as much a question addressed to the spectator as to Monime.

If Xipharès is portrayed such as to elicit our sympathy, so is Monime. We are informed early on of her virtue in her refusal to yield to the king 'une indigne victoire' (51-53). Her resistance on this occasion has been good preparation for her act of defiance against Pharnace in Act I, scene 3, and against Mithridate in Act IV, scene 4. But Monime also displays modesty, as evidenced in her first approach to Xipharès. Although Mithridate's betrothed, her opening speech to Xipharès is a model of deference and discretion (133-162). Her admiration for him leads her to see herself as subordinate and unassuming:

> Songez depuis quel jour ces funestes appas
> Firent naître un amour qu'ils ne méritaient pas...   (681-82)

This attitude of submission is present, paradoxically, even at her moment of greatest resistance when she recognises the debt of gratitude she owes the king for raising her above her previously lowly status (1323-28). Such self-control at a crucial stage of the action is obviously designed to elicit our admiration, in direct contrast to Mithridate at the same point.

Monime is of course anything but dishonourable. To begin with, she emphasises very forcefully her lineage to Pharnace in Act 1, scene 3 (248-50). Her past actions have been entirely informed by a sense of duty since, from the day she wore Mithridate's crown, 'Je renonçai, Seigneur, à ce prince, à moi-même' (1331-32). She evinces considerable concern for her reputation in her preparedness to renounce Xipharès for a second time (697). Later Monime accuses Mithridate of having violated her honour (1350-54). How strange, then, to discover that Monime is capable of such an emotion as hatred (150, 153, 647), although she utters no words which could remotely be considered hateful. One cannot help feeling that Monime overstates her position in portraying herself as 'Tison de la discorde, et fatale furie' (1491).

Mithridate is unquestionably the most well prepared-for character in the play, especially since Xipharès and Pharnace have reason to remind themselves of his attributes on hearing of his return. The king is characterised by his ferocity, particularly when pressed by misfortune (343-44). But an important qualification accompanies one aspect of Pharnace's description (it is indeed interesting that Xipharès is rarely required to portray his father solely in an unfavourable light): 'Rarement l'amitié désarme sa colère' (347). This has an important dramatic consequence later in the play. His cruelty has long been attested to, since we learn that two other sons have been sacrificed to his suspicious inclination (349-50). Of particular concern to his two sons, however, will be his 'jalouse fureur' which will determine his behaviour once he suspects one of them of loving Monime. Xipharès warns the latter of the extremes of cruelty to which 'Mithridate jaloux s'est souvent emporté' (1206). Another aspect of his character we learn of at an early stage is his deviousness, evidenced in his 'dangereux détours' and 'trompeuses adresses', again information supplied by Pharnace (369-72). But Xipharès too is aware of Mithridate's past acts of cruelty, of his 'cruelles amours' and his 'jalouses tendresses' which 'Ont pris soin d'assurer la mort de ses maîtresses' (88).

The details others provide concerning the king are subsequently confirmed by his own actions. His suspicious nature unfolds in his reaction to the presence of his two sons in Nymphée (although here his suspicions are correct) (475). He is certainly imperious and brusque in his manner, as in his interview with Arbate and the greeting he gives his sons in Act II, scene 2. His treatment of Monime in Acts II-IV not only testifies to his cruel streak, as does his command that she take poison, but also to the deviousness mentioned earlier. He clearly perceives himself as an object of fear since, as he tells us, the Bosphorus has seen him more than once 'Ramener la terreur du fond de ses marais' (770). Set against this is his undoubted valour and tenacity in forty years of war and conquest. Mithridate is also capable of love. Pharnace admits that Mithridate distinguishes Xipharès by 'l'amour qu'il vous porte' but warns him at the same time that this may not save his life: 'Sa haine va toujours plus loin que son amour' (354-55). But the king's love has not always been open; Mithridate speaks of his 'tendresse cachée' for his son (468) almost as if affection of this sort were a weakness. It could be argued here that Mithridate's positive qualities are as important as his misdeeds, thus reducing the element of differentiation between Mithridate and Xipharès. While it is indeed true that Xipharès expresses admiration for his father on a number of occasions, this admiration is, however, more integral to our response to Xipharès himself than to Mithridate, as will become clear at a later stage of this chapter. Moreover, despite Mithridate's stature and heroism, it is difficult, in view of his past and present behaviour, to evaluate him in his own words as 'Ennemi des Romains et *de la tyrannie*' (1655, my italics).

The nature of Racinian tragedy, however, does not permit characters to remain statically defined by the particular attributes even frequently ascribed to them. Rather these attributes function as a measure of the extent to which the characters change or develop in the course of the play. In this way, such changes contribute directly to the movement of the action. In the case of Monime, we witness a gradual growth in stature, at least up to the end of Act IV. The discreet and self-effacing woman of Act II demonstrates ultimately a strength of mind and a capacity for defiance which culminates in her refusal to obey Mithridate. She herself perceives the transformation in her character:

Jugez-en, puisque ainsi je vous ose parler,
Et m'emporte au-delà de cette modestie
Dont jusqu'à ce moment je n'étais point sortie.   (1362-64)

The most interesting case of a character suddenly faced
with a consciousness of difference from his former self is that
of Mithridate. His consternation at Monime's behaviour in
Act IV, scene 4 is such that he is reduced to a 'lâche silence'
(1379). Cowardliness is the last attribute Mithridate would
expect to recognise in himself. Moreover, the king, whose
cruelty is frequently referred to, goes as far as to accuse
himself of being too cruel to Monime (1381-82). A moment
later, his self-interrogation, 'Qui suis-je? Est-ce Monime? Et
suis-je Mithridate?' (1383), evinces a genuine process of disorientation. His monologue as a whole reflects a hesitation to
which he is entirely unaccustomed (1407-1408). At the level
of character, such a process is dramatically important because
it reveals to what extent the attributes according to which the
characters have operated in the past and upon which they
have been able to rely are of limited use when they are
confronted with unforeseen and unprecedented situations ('O
Monime! ô mon fils! inutile courroux!', 1409). Long-standing
characteristics are negated in a moment. Moreover, however
much Mithridate attempts to regain his former self, the
situation can never quite revert to what it was before. In the
case of character as in the case of language, the irreversible is
a *sine qua non* of tragic action.

We are confronted here with the idea of characters in
crisis who face moments of self-interrogation to which
straight-forward answers are not necessarily forthcoming. An
important factor in the circumstances of crisis which charac-
terise Racinian plays is therefore the emotional strength
required to deal with them. Characters do not always possess
the self-confidence or confidence in the self they know to be
required. Monime is especially conscious of this, however
much she believes in her virtue. Foreshadowing the results of
her encounter with Mithridate in Act III, scene 5 she warns
Xipharès that his presence makes her especially vulnerable:

'De mes faibles efforts ma vertu se défie' (728). This very interview illustrates her position:

> Plus je vous parle, et plus, trop faible que je suis,
> Je cherche à prolonger le péril que je fuis.   (741-42)

Such weakness therefore requires support:

> Dans ce dessein, vous-même, il faut me soutenir,
> Et de mon faible cœur m'aider à vous bannir.   (701-702)

Awareness of vulnerability does not, as all Racinian tragedy shows, result in a display of strength. Rather a character tends to rely on avoiding difficult situations. Nor is the support which another character may give always available. Hence, characters find themselves facing potential catastrophe alone, deprived of all but their own resources. This form of isolation, of exposure, is a constituent element of tragedy. Monime finds herself in this position in Act III, scene 5 and falls precisely into the trap Mithridate has set her, thus succumbing to the weakness she has mentioned to Xipharès. She describes herself later as 'trop facile à me laisser tromper' (1145). What is most crucial, however, is that she has been caught off her guard: 'Le cruel est venu surprendre ma tendresse' (1232). Her efforts to suppress her love have been to no avail. Indeed Monime's confidence was excessive in allowing herself to believe in her ability to sustain this suppression. She complains to Mithridate:

> Ce feu que dans l'oubli je croyais étouffé...
> Vos détours l'ont surpris...   (1342-44)

I have already commented on the way in which Mithridate's former self fails to assist him in the unprecedented situation he now faces. Indeed some hint of a reason for his disorientation is adumbrated early in the play when Racine makes 'tendresse' rhyme with 'faiblesse'. A further indication of weakness in Mithridate's situation occurs in his monologue deploring his 'inutile courroux'. His attempt to persuade

himself of the need to preserve Xipharès and give him
Monime reveals in its failure the vulnerability of his character at that moment:

> Vains efforts qui ne font que m'instruire
> Des faiblesses d'un cœur qui cherche à se séduire!
> (1403-1404)

It is in the nature of tragedy that an awareness of weakness
arrives too late to be of any real assistance. Awareness itself is
futile.

But Racine's tragedies are not concerned only with 'faiblesse'. There are crucial moments, whose rarity enhances
their value and dramatic appeal, when 'faiblesse' is transcended and a character assumes a strength, usually of defiance. This strength of character does not come easily. It
requires effort and validates even more forcefully the forces
ranged against it. Monime's carefully managed silence provides one example (411-12). This statement is echoed later
when, in order to wrest herself from Xipharès's presence,
Monime declares: 'Il faut pourtant, il faut se faire violence'
(743). The culmination of her effort occurs in her refusal to
marry Mithridate. Her strength of purpose is clearly stated:
'Mais le dessein est pris; rien ne peut m'ébranler' (1361).
Such a position, however heroic, has not been achieved
without cost. Monime's modesty, so vital a part of her virtue,
has been breached.

So far I have been mostly concerned with the characters'
qualities and the way they contribute to the action. In his
preface to *Bérénice* Racine argued that the requirements of
tragedy are 'que l'action en soit grande, et que les acteurs en
soient héroïques'. 'Heroic' contains an ambiguity, for it could
refer simply to historical or legendary status, or to the
qualities demanded of a hero. In the light of many of the
points I have just raised, it will now be useful to devote some
space to the notion of 'heroism' in *Mithridate*. Obviously the
notion of rank is easily satisfied. But what of heroic qualities?

Both Xipharès and Mithridate are proven in battle, the
latter having fought for a lifetime against Rome, being the last

to resist it. But we do not see the king at the height of his
powers. In Act III he speaks of 'Tout l'âge et le malheur que
je traîne avec moi' (1038). On several occasions he refers to
himself as a fugitive (e.g. 759). Furthermore the severity of his
defeat and the confusion of his army have already defined the
limits of heroism (447). Nor does Mithridate's heroic status
exclude misdeeds, a number of which have already been
alluded to. It seems that he has ruled his domestic affairs with
the same ferocity as he has fought his battles. Xipharès warns
Monime:

> Vous dépendez ici d'une main violente,
> Que le sang le plus cher rarement épouvante... (1203-1204)

*Mithridate* raises two questions in particular regarding the
heroic status of the characters. The first involves the notion
of derogation, where the actions or situation of the characters
could be seen to tarnish their reputation as heroes. One
element of such a notion is Mithridate's cruelty. Another is
his inability to impose his authority over his domestic situation, which he himself considers as shameful. Following
Monime's act of defiance, the king reflects on how the
Romans would now perceive his reputation:

> Et vous, heureux Romains, quel triomphe pour vous,
> Si vous saviez ma honte, et qu'un avis fidèle
> De mes lâches combats vous portât la nouvelle! (1410-12)

The circumstances surrounding his relationship with
Monime reflect the shame of his military defeat (839-40).

The second question concerns the trickery and dissimulation which all the characters indulge in at some stage. This
theme opens the play, the news of Mithridate's death having
been a ploy on his part to elude capture. It is moreover an
integral part of his nature as described by Pharnace. But he is
not the first in the play to deceive. Arbate deliberately
conceals the truth about Xipharès (497-98). Later Monime
urges Xipharès to discover a means to avoid her company
and leave Nymphée: 'Inventez des raisons qui puissent

l'éblouir' (722). This is even regarded by Monime as the mark
of a hero: 'D'un héros tel que vous c'est là l'effort suprême'
(723). He is further urged to find a persuasive means 'pour
vous trahir vous-même' (724), which 'l'amour fait inventer
aux vulgaires amants' (726), a rather strange intrusion into
the tragic context. Xipharès is just saved from telling an
untruth by Mithridate's interruption after Pharnace has revealed his brother's interest in Monime (999). Xipharès in his
turn urges Monime to pretend in her attitude to Mithridate
(1212).

The major act of dissimulation is that of Mithridate in Act
III, scene 5, the 'artifice' which will reveal Monime's love for
Xipharès. It is as if the king were conscious of the indignity
of his behaviour by his need to justify the trap: it is worthy of
Monime and Xipharès because they have betrayed him
(1030-31). But our assurance of their innocence in love
alienates us from Mithridate's point of view. Not only does
the king trap her on this occasion but decides to continue his
deceit further (1126) and is actually caught out by Monime in
Act IV, scene 4. The consequences of his first act of deceit for
Mithridate's heroic status are raised by Phœdime who, reas-
suring Monime, asks: 'Un grand Roi descend-il jusqu'à cet
artifice?' (1148).

Racine, however, skilfully rescues what appears as merely
culpable by ensuring that Mithridate, in the way I have
pointed out in Chapter 3, reveals a truth in the very act of
concealing the real reasons for his dissimulation. This is
equally true of Xipharès who, while concealing from Mithridate the real reason for his desire to leave Nymphée, repeats
words of praise we have previously heard him utter when he
tries to persuade Mithridate that it is more expedient that he,
Xipharès, should go to Rome while the king remains in the
Bosphorus (920 seq.). There is no doubt that Xipharès's
praise of his father is sincere.

Such dissimulation would nonetheless seem to contradict
tragic dignity in some way, especially if we attempt to locate
in *Mithridate* the 'tristesse majestueuse' which Racine regards
as constituting 'tout le plaisir de la tragédie'. Dissimulation in
fact is to be found frequently in the plays (*Britannicus,*

*Bajazet, Iphigénie, Phèdre* and *Athalie*). It is not always, however, blameworthy since it may at least have honourable intentions. It allows perhaps for the possibility of survival, a survival in many cases doomed anyway, as in *Bajazet* and *Phèdre*. Survival is a vital issue in *Mithridate*. In fact, as I shall now argue, the survival of Monime and Xipharès further redeems the heroic perspective of the play.

Bernard Weinberg, in *The Art of Jean Racine,* analyses the tragedy from a point of view somewhat different from my own. He regards Mithridate as epic rather than dramatic in nature, since it is, in his opinion, constructed 'according to a schematism that permits the "display" of Mithridate's life and character' (*35,* p. 191). Certainly, Weinberg continues, Racine demonstrates the king's weakness as well as his strength, his vice as well as his virtue, in both actions and passions. But this critic excludes Xipharès and Monime as an alternative focus of the action because the central figure of the king is so dominant that the fate of Monime and Xipharès is subordinate to Mithridate's career of conquest and revenge. I do not believe that such a view of the play is justified.

In the first place our emotional focus is centred on the young couple rather than on Mithridate himself. At only one point in the play is there a case for making the king a truly moving character and that is towards the end of Act IV. Even at the denouement we are more relieved at the survival of Xipharès and Monime (after all she is the object of the 'pathétique' in the play) than sorrowful at Mithridate's death. Secondly, Monime is more important than Weinberg allows since on two occasions her defiance demonstrates a strong Racinian theme, the limits of tyranny over individuals who have the courage to refuse (Andromaque, Junie, Bajazet, Joad). Thirdly, the tragedy develops a parallel drama; the decline of Mithridate as a conqueror (surely the emphasis of Racine), and the survival and panegyric of Xipharès as a worthy successor to his father.

The third point is evident from the very first scene of the play. This provides the spectator with a wholly sympathetic Xipharès, whose many qualities I have enumerated when

examining the notion of character differentiation. He is mod-
est (seeking only his own inheritance, 19-20), brave (70-80),
and above all innocent, for not only did he love Monime
before his father, but he also redeemed himself after his
mother's treachery (61 seq.). From this moment we never lose
sight of Xipharès's qualities as they are perceived by others.
Monime regards him as 'tout plein de vertus, tout brillant de
gloire' (400); Phœdime refers to him as 'ce héros aimable'
(403). Mithridate frequently praises Xipharès. Such is
Racine's urgency to establish the basis for Xipharès's exoner-
ation that Mithridate is made to repeat information already
given when he speaks of his son's devotion to his duty in
denying 'une mère infidèle' (471-72). Further adumbration of
later events comes in Mithridate's intention to reward his son
(509-10). Ironically, when he misunderstands Monime's reaction in Act II, scene 4, the king admonishes her for not
preferring Xipharès, 'ce fils, en effet digne de votre estime'
(600).

Most importantly, however, and this constitutes a crucial
aspect of the action, Mithridate, in the early stages of the
play, expresses his relief that Xipharès does not present
himself as a rival (514), echoing Xipharès's earlier statement
that, after his mother's treachery, 'Je ne regardai plus mon
rival dans mon père' (68). Later Mithridate learns that
Xipharès is indeed a rival (1009). It is not a rivalry to which
we are indifferent, for the dice have been loaded against
Mithridate. Not only does Racine mark Monime's preference
for Xipharès by underlining the king's cruelty and misdeeds,
the last of which is his order that Monime take poison, but
Xipharès is more successful in fighting off the Romans. His
physical prowess is the culmination of our admiration for
him. At the end, as Arbate reports, Xipharès 'vit chargé de
gloire' (1558). Xipharès maintains our good opinion of him
until the end by the grief he displays at his father's agony
(1627).

So thematically *Mithridate* also displays the life and
character of Xipharès in portraying him as the successor to
his father. But he will not be so in quite the way Mithridate
envisages. The king sees his son as 'un autre moi-même'

(1067), the heir to an empire and a name 'qui va renaître en lui' (1069-70). Mithridate's last words are 'Venez et recevez l'âme de Mithridate' (1696). But Xipharès is unquestionably more exemplary than his father. It is an untainted hero who lives on to continue the struggle of Mithridate who, however great, is himself stained by the blood of his past unworthy actions.

This analysis of Xipharès in no way reduces of course the dramatic strength of Mithridate as a character. He is after all the focus of power in the play in terms of his ability to condemn or save the other characters. I have indicated in Chapter 4 how he dominates the play, even when absent from the stage. Such is the case before he even returns to Nympheé and in Act V, when both Monime's cup of poison and reports from the battlefield remind us of Mithridate's redoubtable personality. My intention has been rather to explore ways in which the text seems to provide a problematic view of Mithridate's heroism. As I shall now show, the king's relationship with Monime demonstrates another aspect of the manner in which he imposes himself upon the dramatic action.

Power, as we have seen in the previous discussion and in other chapters, is indeed a theme present on many levels in *Mithridate,* not least on that of love. Here authority is first of all established by the king's preoccupation with possessing Monime as an object. The very physical appearance of Monime testifies to this:

> Et vous portez, Madame, un gage de ma foi
> Qui vous dit tous les jours que vous êtes à moi.   (541-42)

The authoritarian aspect of Mithridate's relationship with Monime is also expressed in the obligations imposed on her by virtue of being an object of possession:

> Ne songez maintenant qu'à répondre à ma flamme.
> Songez que votre cœur est un bien qui m'est dû.   (1280-81)

At his final moment Mithridate clings to Monime as his
'bien': '...souffrez que je vous donne' (1672). But even Mithridate is able to recognise the limits of possession, which are
exemplified by the refusal of the partner to become an *object*
of desire:

> Ainsi, prête à subir un joug qui vous opprime,
> Vous n'allez à l'autel que comme une victime;
> Et, moi, tyran d'un cœur qui se refuse au mien,
> Même en vous possédant je ne vous devrai rien.   (551-54)

Love indeed demands, commands irrespective of the will of
the partner to obey. The demands made upon one character
are based on another's feelings. Hence a transference of
feeling takes place in a character's mind, as when Mithridate
assumes in the case of Monime that 'Vous devez à ce jour dès
longtemps vous attendre' (540). This may be true but not in
the sense that the king means it. The 'foi mutuelle' he refers
to is his own construct, things as they should be. The
isolation of the self is illustrated by the imbalance of 'Ma
gloire loin d'ici, *vous et moi* nous appelle' (544). Such strong
belief in a partnership whose existence cannot in fact be
substantiated leads to a sense of shock and dismay when a
character is disabused. Mithridate's response is to accuse
Monime of ingratitude (1285-88). Monime must now redeem
herself by feeling an emotion she eventually refuses to feel
(1321-22). Mithridate can have recourse only to his status
and to his stature as a means to persuade Monime of her
crime (559 seq.). But this argument is in itself no longer valid.
Hence Mithridate's desperate appeal to Monime that she
remind herself of what he once was.

Passion, then, is directly related to power. Mithridate
*commands* Monime to love him. His first speech to her
contains an element of threat (539). Monime can respond
only on the level of obedience not of emotion (550). In the
final scene he still attempts to command her feelings, albeit
this time in the right direction:

...et tous ces vœux que j'exigeais de vous,
Mon cœur pour Xipharès vous les demande tous.   (1673-74)

Essentially, however, in the context of the power relations involved in Racinian passion, there is only one alternative to 'plaire', and that is 'tyranniser' (556-57).

The theme of power is important too at the level of character and action. To what degree do the characters themselves control the action, and to what degree do their qualities contribute to or undermine that control? How free are the characters to act? Xipharès, for example, thwarts Pharnace in his plans by returning to Nymphée. Monime also contributes to Pharnace's failure to assert himself as a ruler by refusing his offer of marriage. The power of all three to establish their authority over the situation evaporates with Mithridate's return. The obvious pattern might be that he, with all the ruthlessness we have been led to expect, will influence events in his favour, or at least destroy those who obstruct him. But Mithridate soon learns that power is not the equivalent of control.

This is not necessarily owing to the forces ranged against him, although they are considerable. As he repeatedly states himself, he is a defeated king in external terms. The Romans have put him to flight and reduced him to immobility. He is reduced also, it would appear, to words. His inaction is transparent in the very idea of a march on Rome, where even Xipharès's enthusiasm cannot conceal the unreality of the project. Eventually Mithridate's own character compounds his external defeat. His actions in the play, true to the form of his past actions, lead to the loss of control over his own household.

Monime does not spare the king's feelings in specifying to him that he himself is responsible for her refusal to marry him (1339-40). His ruthlessness, his recourse to dissimulation and trickery have served only to encourage opposition. Consequently, the power relations between him and Monime are now reversed. Monime's refusal denies the king power over her, while admittedly she is aware of the physical danger she exposes herself to (1358 seq.). Mithridate's inaction results in

his desperate cry: 'O Monime! ô mon fils! inutile courroux!'
(1409). Even when he has given orders that she take poison,
Monime undermines the order and his authority, not by
refusing but by accepting the drink as her own act in expi-
ation of her betrayal of Xipharès (she has already tried to
hang herself with the diadem, 1521-22).

Of course, external events reassert themselves at the end
of Act IV. But even here the emphasis is not entirely on these
events wresting control from the king. Rather our attention is
drawn to Mithridate unable to control his own death. He
attempts suicide by poison but fails, because he has become
immune, having previously taken poison to avoid attempts
on his life (1414). Falling on his sword provides no immediate relief: 'Mais la mort fuit encor sa grande âme trompée'
(1604). This is of course opportune because Mithridate then
rescinds the order given previously to Monime.

Undoubtedly, however, the dramatic action in Act V is
unsatisfactory. Monime may survive, Xipharès may succeed
Mithridate, but the action itself remains fairly static except
for reports of Mithridate's and Xipharès's valiant resistance.
This is because Monime's power to act has lain in her refusal
and nothing more. Xipharès and Mithridate have by now
disappeared from the immediate orbit of the stage. In any
case, Xipharès is throughout *Mithridate* unwilling to act
against his father, even urging Monime to feign cooperation
with the king. In Act V, all the characters are deprived of the
possibility of action. Mithridate can only go back on an order
already given. Racine has deprived the action of its force once
the power relations between the two active individuals are
reversed in Act IV. The internal dynamic of character has
exhausted itself.

# Conclusion

$M$ *ITHRIDATE*'S status as a tragedy has always given rise to debate. Raymond Picard regards it as 'peut-être...la tragédie la moins *tragique* de Racine' (*25*, I, p. 614), and according to Alain Viala it is 'd'essence peu tragique à proprement parler' (*26*, p. 444). Such a view rests partly on the 'glorious' end of Mithridate himself, which inspires 'admiration' rather than the emotions usually associated with tragic endings. My analysis of the tragedy's denouement therefore runs counter to the projection of the play as possessing epic rather than tragic qualities.

I do not believe either that careful examination of the play can sustain the widely stated opinion that *Mithridate* is Racine's most 'Cornelian' tragedy. Certainly, as Picard observes (without himself specifically stating this opinion), 'Faire son devoir, conserver son estime, c'est là le but de chacun de ces héros' (*25*, ibid). But, as I have shown, the characters' solutions, and in some cases their actions, are far from Cornelian (whatever that may mean).

*Mithridate* is not without tragic quality and, of course, Racine himself argued that tragedy is not necessarily defined by its ending. The play contains the relentless and even cruel exposure of its characters whose private feelings are forced into the open. The pattern of revelation is always consequential, potentially or actually, either in placing others and oneself in danger (Xipharès, Monime) or in leading to painful discovery (Mithridate). Revelations of the sort I have described, particularly in chapter 3, also demonstrate the irreversible nature of the Racinian tragic crisis. It is true that, unlike other tragedies of Racine, the situation in *Mithridate* is retrievable. But this does not *necessarily* redound to the credit of the king.

Whatever the flaws of *Mithridate,* and in some instances
they are considerable, the play demonstrates the overall
significance of Racinian tragedy, namely that if passion
destroys individuals, it does not destroy order. Moreover,
Racine's tragedies are never complete without a compensa-
tory force which provides an emotional equilibrium in the
play. In *Mithridate,* this is provided by Monime, around
whose immobility the play revolves. Her attempt at self-
control, while threatened in Act V, reveals that reason and
emotion are contiguous in the human mind, where each
survives the other. As Brecht once remarked, in what could
be an eminently suitable comment about our response to
Racinian tragedy, 'in the theatre one thinks feelingly and one
feels thoughtfully'. Indeed, Racinian tragedy, more than any
other, despite its apparent view of the disruptive character of
humanity, makes the case for the pleasure of the emotions, a
pleasure defined by our intelligence of that experience.

# Bibliography

1. Barthes, R., *Sur Racine* (Paris, Seuil, 1963).
2. ——, *Critique et vérité* (Paris, Seuil, 1966).
3. Butler, P., *Classicisme et baroque dans l'œuvre de Racine* (Paris, Nizet, 1959).
4. Doubrovsky, S., *Pourquoi la nouvelle critique? Critique et objectivité* (Paris, Mercure de France, 1966).
5. Drown, N. K., *Racine: Meditations on his Poetic Art* (s.l.) (s.n.) 1982.
6. Edwards, M., *La Tragédie racinienne* (Paris, La Pensée Universelle, 1972).
7. France, P., *Racine's Rhetoric* (Oxford, O.U.P., 1965).
8. Goldmann, L., *Le Dieu caché* (Paris, Gallimard, 1955).
9. ——, *Racine* (Paris, L'Arche, 1970).
10. Gutwirth, M., *Jean Racine: un itinéraire poétique* (Montreal, Presses de l'Université, 1970).
11. Hubert, J. D., *Essai d'exégèse racinienne: les secrets témoins* (Paris, Nizet, 1956).
12. Lapp, J. C., *Aspects of Racinian Tragedy* (Toronto, University Press, 1964).
13. Maland, D., *Culture and Society in Seventeenth-Century France* (London, Batsford, 1970).
14. Maulnier, T., *Racine* (Paris, Gallimard, 1947).
15. Mauron, C., *L'Inconscient dans l'œuvre et la vie de Racine* (Gap, Annales de la Faculté de Lettres d'Aix, 1957).
16. Morel, J., *La Tragédie* (Paris, Armand Colin, 1964).
17. Mourgues, O. de, *Autonomie de Racine* (Paris, Corti, 1967).
18. ——, *Racine: or, the Triumph of Relevance* (Cambrige, C.U.P., 1967).
19. Muecke, D. C., *Irony* (London, Methuen, 1970).
20. Niderst, A., *Les Tragédies de Racine* (Paris, Nizet, 1975).
21. O'Regan, M., *The Mannerist Aesthetic: a Study of Racine's 'Mithridate'* (Bristol, University of Bristol Printing Unit, 1980).
22. Parish, R., '"Un calme si funeste": Some Types of Silence in Racine', *French Studies,* XXXIV (October 1980), 385-400.
23. Picard, R., *La Carrière de Jean Racine* (Paris, Gallimard, 1961).
24. ——, *Nouvelle Critique ou nouvelle imposture* (Paris, Pauvert, 1965).
25. Racine, J., *Œuvres,* ed. R. Picard, Pléiade, 2 vols (Paris, Gallimard, 1960).

26. Racine, J., *Théâtre complet,* ed. J. Morel et A. Viala (Paris, Garnier, 1980).
27. ———, *Mithridate,* ed. G. Rudler, Blackwell's French Texts (Oxford, Blackwell, 1960).
28. ———, *Mithridate,* ed. J. Boullé et C. Labrosse (Paris, Bordas, 1965).
29. ———, *Mithridate,* ed. M. Brunelle, Nouveaux Classiques Larousse (Paris, Larousse, 1967).
30. Scherer, J., *Racine, et/ou la cérémonie* (Paris, P.U.F., 1982).
31. Spitzer, L., 'Racine's Classical *Piano'* in *Essays on Seventeenth-Century French Literature,* translated, edited and with an introduction by D. Bellos (Cambridge, C.U.P., 1983), pp. 3-113.
32. Starobinski, J., 'La Poétique du regard' in *L'Œil vivant* (Paris, Gallimard, 1961).
33. Styan, J. L., *The Elements of Drama* (Cambridge, C.U.P., 1960).
34. Truchet, J., *La Tragédie classique en France* (Paris, P.U.F., 1975).
35. Weinberg, B., *The Art of Jean Racine* (Chicago, University Press of Chicago, 1969).

# CRITICAL GUIDES TO FRENCH TEXTS

*edited by*
Roger Little, Wolfgang van Emden, David Williams